odd
jobs

THE TIMES

odd
jobs

Unusual
ways to earn a living

2nd edition

SIMON KENT

**KOGAN
PAGE**

First published in 2000
Second edition published in 2002

Apart from any fair dealing for the purposes of research or private study, or criticism or review, as permitted under the Copyright, Designs and Patents Act 1988, this publication may only be reproduced, stored or transmitted, in any form or by any means, with the prior permission in writing of the publishers, or in the case of reprographic reproduction in accordance with the terms and licences issued by the CLA. Enquiries concerning reproduction outside these terms should be sent to the publishers at the undermentioned address:

Kogan Page Limited
120 Pentonville Road
London N1 9JN

British Library Cataloguing in Publication Data

A CIP record for this book is available from the British Library.

ISBN 0 7494 3705 7

Typeset by Saxon Graphics Ltd, Derby
Printed and bound in Great Britain by Clays Ltd, St Ives plc

Contents

Contents

And So
To Work

Warning! This is not a careers book. This book will not tell you what to do with the rest of your life and at no point will it tell you how to write a good CV.

However, this book will help you find a fun, off-the-wall job and, moreover, a job that you want to do. Steering clear of Careers Centre pamphlets, avoiding Job Centre notice boards and careers fairs, it takes a less-beaten track, heading for out of the way places, territories you may have thought of only in passing and some you may never have considered.

While this book clearly features certain jobs and roles you may want to pursue, the search does not end there. Each section begins with an introductory piece that covers certain aspects of the job market and suggests ways into the workplace. Even the job descriptions themselves are not always limited to one single activity, exploring instead related possibilities and encouraging you to think laterally about what you can do.

If you have an interest, a hobby, an obsession or a passion for something, this book can help you turn that positive energy into a livelihood. If you can name what you want to do for a living but everyone tells you to be realistic or says, 'No one will pay you to do that!', this book will put you on the right track to realising your goal.

Too good to be true? Not really! Today's workplace is an incredibly diverse and fast-moving place. There is always a place for the entrepreneur – the person who spots a new opportunity and has the determination to follow it through.

Imagination, energy and enthusiasm are prized above academic achievement, company loyalty and kowtowing to corporate structures. The Internet has not only introduced a whole new media and business area in which people can work, it has brought together formerly disparate individuals, creating new marketing opportunities and causing traditional business to reinvent itself. Add to this an increase in leisure spend for many people, and what do you get? A whole pile of odd jobs.

In researching this book, I found that many people involved in these jobs did not perceive their work to be outlandish. It was also clear that very often there were elements of the work that were run of the mill and amounted to everyday basic grind, which results in long hours to be worked and not enough money in the pay packet. However, what makes these jobs special is that they tap into areas of workers' personalities – parts of their lives that would be important even if they weren't doing this job for a living. Therefore, the motivation they experience is not connected to monetary recognition or the conventional trappings of status, but to something much more powerful – something that means the hours, the hard work and the grind is more than worth it.

The trick to finding this kind of work is to think laterally. Burn the rulebooks and don't take 'no' for an answer! Think about what you want to do, what you can do and the context in which you can do it. Think about the people who might pay you to do it and those you might need to help you in that position. Think of yourself as fitting in to a supply and demand chain: who are the customers who will want your service or product, and who are the suppliers who can give you the raw materials? How will what you do add value to your customers' lives?

Frequently, these jobs require self-employment or even the establishment of a new business. This demands a whole new set of skills and self-discipline from you in order to work alone, to attract customers and ensure the business survives. It is difficult but extremely rewarding work, and it can mean going to work has simply become a way of being paid to play.

Technology has radically changed the world of work, and it has also altered the game of job hunting. The amount of information now accessible through the World Wide Web is inconceivable. For the job seeker, or anyone who wants to know more about one particular area of work, a first step is to find a good search engine and type in a few keywords. The results could be life changing.

Jobbing it for enjoyment

Work does not need to be a hardship. In fact, work can be fun! If you play your cards right, you may never have a single day's work that isn't exciting, fulfilling and satisfying. With a little imagination and a lot of enthusiasm, you can line up a whole range of perfect jobs – activities you enjoy so much that the pay packet is simply the icing on the cake.

Having spent so many years in the education system, you may feel it's time to prove your skills in the real world and show what you really can do. But is this possible by immediately finding a lifelong employer who wants you to contribute to their firm in their way? Having spent so long gaining knowledge and honing your skills, do you really want to take a position that may only exercise you in a few of those areas? Why should work be a place where you leave your imagination behind, or even your personality? Checking in for a day's work should not mean clicking in to the same old routine; it should mean triggering your motivation and excitement.

Right now you have the ideal opportunity to experiment in the workplace – to find different things to do, take on new challenges and play a wide variety of roles. You can take jobs simply because you like the look of them. You can take seasonal work to suit your lifestyle: outdoor or travel-related work during the summer, indoor work during the winter. You can try out a physically demanding job to see whether you are suited to it, and then try something more technical or office-based so that you are able to compare the two. You do not need to commit yourself to a long-term contract but can determine for yourself how long you want to stay with each employer. After the prescriptive lifestyle of full-time education, you are now in charge of what you do – and no one else.

Full-time employment takes up a lot of time – about a third of your life will be spent working. And that will still affect the other two-thirds – and not just by giving you the means with which you can live. It may demand overtime and fill your head with problems and issues you'd rather not think about on your days off. It may determine your leisure time, how you dress and how you speak. When you meet other people, your job will be one of the primary methods by which they will identify you. Trying out a range of jobs will give you an insight into all of these identities to find the one that suits you best.

Certainly you will need to work to earn money in order to be able to live but work should not be a purely financial transaction. Work should give you a full range of life experiences, such as working with different people and initiating and completing your own projects – thrills and spills in equal measure. At this early stage in your career you are perfectly placed to demand those experiences from your working life. A few years down the line, your priorities and responsibilities may have changed, but as a newly qualified entrant to the job market the world is your playground.

There have never been more ways of tracking down fun, interesting and bizarre things to do for a living than there are today. The communications revolution has made the world a smaller place and established all kinds of links between people and organisations that simply did not exist before. The Internet can put you in touch with people from all over the world, people who can offer advice and opportunities, and people who will be more than happy to be your future customers. Think globally in your search for work. You may not fancy working the photo-copier in an office in your local town, but what if, as soon as you have finished, you could walk out into the sunshine and relax on Bondi Beach?

Prioritise your job search according to what you want to do, as much as by what you are qualified to do. Volunteer your services wherever practical or necessary and work for the experience you will gain. Find people you want to work with rather than having your social circle forced upon you through work colleagues. Find a job that identifies you as an individual, and highlights your imagination and personality.

So go ahead: pick up the phone and dial the company who has the job you've always wondered about. Find out what skills you need to be a roller skating waiter or waitress in a New York café. Surf the Web and discover what opportunities there are for you as a fire-eating minstrel in Australia. Work hard and work fun.

Getting Technical

Together, the PC and the Internet offer the greatest opportunity for work in the UK today. This is partly because computer use is an everyday part of practically every other industry. No matter what a company does, if it ignores the potential of the Internet – whether as a means of self-promotion or to introduce increased efficiency across internal processes – it ignores a lucrative source of additional revenue. The proliferation of technology in the workplace has itself created a few odd jobs – there are 'chief IT gurus' and 'heads of future technology' in many companies, although in some cases these are simply attempts at glamorising straightforward IT management jobs. At the same time, you could find yourself with a novel position just because of the type of information you handle through IT. You could, for example, design Web pages for an innovative theatre company, or find yourself specifying an IT back office system for a zoo – designed to manage both animals and people.

Demand for Internet skills already outstrips supply – and this situation will remain well into the future – while the proliferation of PCs in every workplace means applicants for all kinds of jobs will be more employable if they can show computer skills. At the same time, an increasing number of new technology platforms – PDAs, handheld devices and WAP technology – means you may find you need to make that theatre company or zoo information compatible over several different formats. The trend is towards convergence of these technologies – a mobile phone which offers Web access, e-mail facilities and the processing power of a handheld device, for example. But whatever future gadgets look like, organisations will want to be able to make their information accessible seamlessly across the media.

The good news for jobseekers is that you do not need to be a high-flying computer science graduate to secure a place in the new technology industry. Provided you can show evidence of your skills – and they are the skills an organisation wants – you can be self-taught. All you need to do is offer employers some great ideas and prove that you can carry out the work they want you to do.

That said, some organisations are becoming increasingly demanding about the recruits they take. Not too long ago, the vast majority of employees in Internet companies had simply transferred from other areas of industry, retraining and mixing IT skills with their previous knowledge – usually marketing, design or communications. Today, there are workers who have spent their whole careers in IT and working with the Internet. They have taken specific courses that give them high level specialist skills and it is these people who are now taking the top roles in the job market. To be sure of success, therefore, newcomers to the industry should be able to offer targeted technology-related skills or qualifications recognised and demanded by the industry.

Throughout the Internet and games market the workplace is split between 'techies' and 'creatives' – those who can program and those who can come up with ideas on what should appear on Web pages and so on. While you will find yourself working in one or other of these areas, the more understanding of both areas you can offer, the higher your value will be in the job market.

Web page designer

The Internet has been recognised as an important business tool and practically every organisation is looking to this medium to carry advertisements, contact details and company information. The opportunities for Web page designers are vast. While some Web programming is fairly easy to understand and execute, good Web designers are at a premium and can charge great sums of money for their work.

Some Web page designers have advertising or marketing backgrounds but designers are appearing who have worked solely with the Internet as their medium. As a result, they understand completely what it can do. While evidence of academic study in this area can be important for some employers, it is more than possible to get a job with a Web design agency on the evidence of ability alone. If you have created your own Web page and employers are impressed with the result, you may be able to convince them to employ you regardless of your qualifications.

The first stage of the work is to pitch ideas for the Web pages to clients. Unlike traditional advertising media – newspapers and TV – Web pages can be updated instantly and the technology is advancing at such a speed that what is possible today is likely to be old hat by next week. Therefore, when presenting a pitch, it is necessary to be clear about exactly what the clients are going to get for their money. If other ideas emerge while working on that page, they should be treated under a separate project. Without this kind of arrangement, designers can find they have worked for many months on a single Web page and received insufficient remuneration.

This applies to the technology you use to create the Web page as much as to the content or interactivity put on the site itself. The popularity of handheld devices and WAP phone technology means companies need to get their message across all these technology platforms. It often falls to the page designer to work out how that information can be formatted for each media.

Obviously, the best Web pages are those that attract large numbers of visitors and keep them there for a long time. Designers need to ensure their sites are 'sticky' to keep people glued to their screens. This can be done using different techniques – interactive features on the site, regular updates and interesting downloads for visitors to use can all help. The Web designer might even create a mailing list where interested visitors can sign up to be informed of any changes made in the future.

There are no standards to the structure or operation of Web design companies, so designers may find themselves working in all sorts of situations – in teams, alone, on long-term projects or small parts of other projects. Designers need to use a wide range of programming languages in order to carry out different tasks on the Web page. The industry has a young and mobile workforce who move from company to company easily, attracted by the variety and type of work on offer as much as by remuneration.

 Highs: Building innovative sites and breaking new ground in design. Cracking a piece of difficult code and finding a way of making a Web site feature easier and quicker to upload.

 Lows: Matching the ideas for Web pages with what is practically possible. There can be long hours of programming to reach deadlines and it is inevitable that you will have to deal with crashing computers and the limits of technology.

Facts, links and trivia

The HTML Writer's Guild is an international association of Web page writers and other people who use HTML – hypertext mark-up language. The organisation originated in the United States but is a 'virtual community', communicating through e-mails, online forums and shared training resources. It currently has 147,000 members in over 150 companies and recently merged with the International Webmaster's Association www.iwanet.org. Its Web site is at http://hwg.org and offers current news from the industry as well as links to training resources. There is also an ongoing Internet-based publication for Web page designers at http://www.wpdfd.com (Web page design for designers) which provides an overview of new technologies used on Web pages as well as occasional hints and tips on programming techniques.

Training for the profession can be taken at any time in your career and is delivered through a wide variety of sources. Local colleges run basic introductory courses to page building – part-time or evening classes. More sophisticated programming requires more substantial study through Higher and Further Education. There are also courses available through the technology companies who pioneer Web technology.

Computer game designer and builder

Home entertainment has become big business as games consoles now bring arcade-style amusements into the living room. There is fierce competition not only among game producers but also between the companies who build the consoles, with technology driving relentlessly towards greater realism in its use of graphics and within each game scenario. The industry needs both creative and technical people to imagine and drive the games forward. As the industry has developed, there has been a shift in entrance requirements with increased preferences for high academic achievers. However, there is room still for the maverick – the genius who has been programming the home computer for years and knows every game inside out. Whatever your background might be you will need to be highly proficient in using C and C++ programming. The reason why C programming is so popular for games is because it is not tied to any particular system requirement. This means the programmer can write one program that will run effectively on diverse systems with different specifications.

The studios where the games are created employ a hierarchy of workers devoted to creating one specific game. The creative director oversees the entire process of putting the game together – from the initial idea for the game through to the final appearance of characters and background, the sound effects and special effects used in the game. Alongside the director is the producer whose job it is to ensure the project is brought in on schedule and within budget. Beneath these two are a team of workers ranging from concept artists, who provide the first visual input into a game, through to the programmers who make the game work and even musicians who write and record the background music and any incidental sound effects. There is frequently compromise involved in the development of a game, as the vision of the game's designers can prove difficult for the programmers to realise.

One of the more junior jobs a technical worker can expect to take on is as a level mapper. In this role programmers map out the area in which the game is played – they assign certain qualities to the 3D space ensuring that characters cannot walk through walls but can open doors and blow up other items. In this way players will not suddenly find that they are able to move through solid objects or travel outside the game.

All workers in the industry, whether designing or programming the intricacies of the game, must have a sound knowledge of the computer games market.

 Highs: Creating new games that can have thousands of people hooked to their games modules.

 Lows: Working to deadlines on this kind of project can be stressful and sometimes the work involves dealing with problems more than it involves being creative.

Facts, links and trivia

Within the creation of games, the two main specialist areas are artwork and music. Relevant degrees in these areas can help but are not essential. It is more important to have a portfolio of demonstration work ready to show potential employers what you can do. For the music element of the game a thorough understanding of the recording and the use of digital sound will be more useful than classical composition. While composers in this area are well paid, they are likely to work on a freelance basis, simply because the music is treated as a separate element to be added towards the end of the game's creation.

'Game On' is part of the Interactive Studios Web site at www.intstudios.co.uk and offers many hints and tips for people who want to get into the games industry. One of its recommendations is that anyone who seriously wants to be involved should start playing as many games as possible. You need to go further than simply knowing how to complete a game and understand what makes it addictive, how the designers have used the interactive potential and how the storyline or scenario for the game has been constructed. For further information and training on C and C++ languages you can try www.cyberdiem.com or check out The Association of C and C++ users at www.accu.org.

When a new game or console is being built, secrecy surrounds the entire project. If a company is going to maximise its return on investment it must keep the technology under wraps and prevent the launch being spoiled by information seeping out about what the game will do. Employees working on such key projects may even be 'cut off' from their co-workers.

Computer games tester

In the early days of the computer games industry, testers did not exist. Faults and bugs within game programs were identified and addressed by the programmers themselves. Today, no new computer game is released until professional game players have rigorously tested it. For this reason, game design studios employ devoted players to play the game thoroughly – trying every part of the game to ensure it works properly and will not crash in spite of everything a player might do during the course of playing. This means playing a game over and over for days at a time, sometimes video-taping the game as it is played in order to capture bugs in the programming as they happen.

Quality assurance (QA) staff carry out this analysis. They will provide feedback on the design of the game, on features such as how easy it is to move through each level to complete the game and how easy the controls are to understand and operate. They may also need to report back on legal issues – games may feature images or sounds that fall under copyright restrictions and must be cleared before the product goes to market.

Therefore, aside from playing games, QA staff need to be good communicators, able to explain problems precisely and to provide useful feedback for the programmers or game designers. They also need to be tactful and diplomatic – a bunch of programmers can take offence at testers who they perceive as just spending all day playing the games and creating problems. QA staff can be employed on a full- or part-time basis at different levels in the industry. They may test games for the game producers – the companies who are creating the products in the first place. They may alternatively test the games for the larger organisations who make the gaming consoles. They may work for one of the international computer giants, ensuring all gaming products using its platform meet a satisfactory standard.

At the bottom end of this ladder – at the creation level of the game for the producing companies – testers will only be required when the product has reached a certain stage of development. They may only be brought in when the game is almost ready for release, and although this can be between six and eight months from the inception of the game, there's no guarantee of length of contract for these workers. In spite of the short-term contracts in this area, it is possible to find work moving around the industry – playing games for different organisations as you go along.

This structure also means testers are brought into the process just when things start to get very stressful – the deadline for launching the game is fast approaching and programmers must deliver a bug-free product in time. The tester can then be one of the people working all hours of the day and night, checking out every part of the game and ensuring modifications are effective.

Knowledge of programming skills can be useful for QA employees so they can suggest solutions to any glitches they encounter, but certainly the most important requirement is a complete and all-encompassing knowledge of the games market. To be effective, the testers must be able to complete levels and games quickly and accurately, particularly if they are trying to pinpoint a specific glitch. If QA players have played similar games, they will be able to feed back on how the new product measures up. There may be certain features or something about the way a games console is used that the new game can incorporate. They can also tell the designers how addictive the game is – a quality that the designers and programmers themselves may find difficult to assess since they have worked on the game for so long.

Highs: You get to play games all day – long before anyone else gets to buy them in the shops.

 Lows: Playing the same game day in, day out for weeks at a time can get tedious, and you should realise that within the industry you are regarded as being at the bottom of the heap.

Facts, links and trivia

Permanently employed testers can make around £15–17K a year and while this is one of the easier areas of the games industry to get involved in, there is still fierce competition at entry level. The role can lead to positions within games design and programming as long as you have the necessary skills and talents.

Testers can work for game developers, console manufacturers and even across PC based games. The latter is the trickiest of testing areas since PCs can have diverse hardware that can conflict with a game programme. To be completely certain of a game's stability and effectiveness, testers need to try the game out with a variety of sound and graphics cards. Even then, a PC game can crash due to external system problems or some chance key combination. Given this, there can still be bugs within a game when it is finally shipped. The Web page www.fatbabies.com is a US based news site for the games industry. It has also been the site for gossip and rumours from testers so is worth checking out to get an idea of what it's like to be in this part of the business.

Chat room host

One of the most popular aspects of the Internet today is the ability to chat in real time with other people from around the world via the computer keyboard. Not only have Internet service providers (ISPs) established their own online communities where users can log on and chat to like-minded people, but many commercial organisations now include a chat room facility on their own Web site. The BBC, for example, includes chat rooms where users can share ideas and comment on recent programmes while ISPs such as Freeserve have a whole host of chat rooms defined by age and interest.

In order to get maximum benefit form this interaction, every chat room has its own rules. These cover aspects such as being polite to other users, not trying to use the chat room to sell a product or service and not to allow the conversation to stray too far from the subject for which the room was designed. While the majority of users follow these, there are a minority who may disregard the rules. There is also the risk that someone in the chat room isn't actually who he or she claims to be and may be using the online environment to deceive other users.

Chat room technology is very difficult to monitor automatically. While there is software that will monitor, filter and censor Web pages according to the content on each page, there is no way suspicious or abusive text conversations can be detected or removed before they are submitted. In addition, the technology behind these rooms will not record the interaction for posterity so anyone who does break the rules may be able to do so without being tracked down. Therefore, in order to monitor proceedings it is necessary to employ a human to watch the interactions and ensure everyone behaves themselves.

Employed by the company running the site, the chat room host has the power to throw people out of the chat rooms as soon as they submit any inappropriate interactions. That contributor can be banned from any further interactions and if the contribution had criminal implications the host may contact their local police computer crime unit in order to find the offender.

For very busy sites, or for those targeted at children, it may be necessary to employ a host around the clock. Different people will take it in turns to monitor activities, perhaps while working on other projects for their employer. Quieter and more adult sites may only need the host to drop in every now and then to check the space is still being used and used properly. Every chat room should have an alert key which users can hit if they are subjected to abusive or disturbing chat. In such an event, the host must respond to the situation immediately, reassuring the victim and taking steps against the abuser.

The host can also be employed to play a proactive part in the conversation within the room. They may invite comment from reticent users or introduce new ideas if the conversation starts to flag. Occasionally, a chat room will be used specifically to enable users to chat with a specialist or celebrity. The interviewee will be open to questions from users and the responses are submitted as conventional chat. Interviewees may decide to type the answers to the questions themselves if they are computer literate, but more often it will be the host's responsibility to transfer the verbal answers to the screen. Either way, the host must facilitate the interaction, ensuring submitted questions are answered in order and that the conversation doesn't become disjointed or confusing.

 Highs: Working in an interactive medium with people from across the world.

 Lows: There may be boring or repetitive conversations which you have to monitor or repeated questions from users. Whatever the space is used for you still need to appear excited and enthusiastic about the subject.

Facts, links and trivia

You only need to go to an ISP site such as www.yahoo.co.uk or www.freeserve.com to see chat rooms in action. There are also dedicated companies such as www.towerchat.com who are taking chat rooms into new areas by allowing users to design their own virtual characters – how they will appear to other users in the chat room. Some companies allow you to open your own chat rooms (if one doesn't already exist to cover your subject) and you can apply to be that room's moderator. Naturally this job will be unpaid but it will offer an experience of the work.

In April 2001 the Government set up a taskforce to tackle Internet safety for children. Their campaign, WISEUP-TOTHEWEB (www.wiseuptotheweb.co.uk) is aimed at giving advice to children and adults on how to make the Web an enjoyable and safe experience. Since chat rooms cannot be censored or filtered in advance, the best way of preventing abuse is to make sure users know what they can do to avoid and counter such situations.

Test pilot

Before a new or modified aircraft can be given over to a commercial or military organisation, it must be tested thoroughly to establish that the vehicle can do what it is meant to without placing the pilot or passengers in peril. While this may immediately conjure up an image of some daredevil pilot, leaping fearlessly into the cockpit of a brand new jet plane and taking it into the wild blue yonder, the job itself requires a substantial amount of planning and basic desk work before and after the flight.

Test pilots are drawn from the ranks of experienced pilots, usually with a military background and always with significant experience of flying a range of craft. They will also have a degree or similar academic qualification in engineering. They will undergo specific training at a test pilot school following a course to sharpen their skills. These courses may be specific to aircraft – for example, fixed or rotary wing – or more general courses in flight test principles and practice.

The use of flight simulation as well as the basic study of aircraft design and engineering means in general test pilots have a fairly clear idea of how a plane will behave once in the air before they get into the cockpit. It is possible to predict aspects such as manoeuvrability, speed and distance while still at the concept stage. However, there will always be new discoveries made in an aircraft's design when it takes to the air with a human pilot at the controls. Moreover, if the craft needs to carry out more complex tasks, such as in-flight refuelling or short-runway landing, it is only by trying this for real that designers can see exactly how the plane performs. By placing such tests early on in the design and build stage of a new aircraft, the designers can address any problems as soon as they arise.

While test pilots are valued for their experience at the controls of a new aircraft, they also need strong technical skills to be able to write up thorough reports on the flight for the plane's designers and engineers to use. Prior to testing they will work with flight test engineers to draw up test procedures and identify how to effectively measure the aircraft's performance. After the tests have been completed the pilots need to write up technical reports on certain aspects of the craft's performance, explaining precisely what happened during set procedures such as a spin or take-off. Sometimes, it can seem that test pilots spends most of their time behind a desk doing this kind of paperwork rather than sitting in the cockpit.

All aircraft are tested according to their destined use. The trials for a multi-engine, multi-crew aircraft will be different to criteria required for a military fighter or for a police helicopter. In each case, the demands of the end user and the environment in which the craft will be used must be factored into any tests created.

 Highs: The thrill of flying an aircraft for the first time and having a direct influence on the future design of this craft and others like it.

 Lows: The amount of analysis and paper work that must be completed before a flight can take place. While this is absolutely crucial in order to maximise pilot safety, it can detract from the experience of flying itself.

Facts, links and trivia

There are six test pilot schools in the United States, France and the UK. They are either military or civilian owned. In the United States there are military schools at Edwards Air Force Base, in the Mojave Desert, California and at Patuxent River, Maryland. This latter is the US Navy Test Pilot School and trains over 70 people every year. The National Test Pilot School, also at

Mojave, is civilian owned. In France there is the Ecole du Personnel Navigant d'Essais et de Reception (EPNER) at Istres while England boasts a military school at Boscombe Down and the civilian owned International Test Pilots School at Woodford.

To be successful in securing training and in getting a good career as a test pilot, you must be prepared to travel, working across continents and for different organisations. More information on the UK's Empire Test Pilot School can be found at http://www.etps.dera.gov.uk. The school is now part of DERA, the Defense Evaluation & Research Agency and you can write to their information service at: ETPS, DERA Boscombe Down, Salisbury, Wiltshire SP4 0JF (tel: 01980 662656).

Pilots tend to be aged mid-20s to early-30s. At this time it's generally thought that they've got over any youthful impetuousness, while still having enough time to repay the training invested in them. Pilots with families should realise they'll need to be mobile too.

Environmental tester

This technical role occurs towards the final stages of the design process in many manufacturing businesses. Essentially, it is the environmental tester's duty to ensure a product is up to the job for which it has been created. Testers are used, for example, to make sure mobile phones can withstand the abuse their owners are likely to inflict on them during everyday use. They consider and analyse children's toys to ensure they are not dangerous. They even simulate conditions in space to ensure satellite craft will operate having endured the experience of being blasted out of the earth's atmosphere on top of a rocket.

Environmental testers may therefore be attached to specific manufacturing companies at the final stages of production. Alternatively they can be part of a general standards assessment company working across a number of different areas, providing analysis and measuring the performance of operations and products from other companies.

It is a very creative role in which technicians carefully study the conditions that the product will be subject to and design suitable experiments to simulate those effects. The technicians then subject the product to those tests – this may be a prototype or the equipment itself. For example, street lighting must still be able to operate regardless of rain, wind and extremes of temperature. The testers will therefore set up the light inside a wind tunnel and see what happens when they subject the light to strong winds over a period of time. They may immerse the lighting shield in water to check for leaks. They will also measure the light levels coming off the fitting and make sure this is suitable for its intended job.

By looking at the way mobile phones are treated – left inside cars, dropped out of pockets and so on – testers can devise comparable temperature tests and drop tests. For the latter, every phone tested is dropped on to concrete from increasing heights and the effects recorded.

Testing technology for use in space holds particular challenges and environmental testers in this field use vacuum chambers and vibrating machines to simulate conditions during the launch and once the craft is in orbit.

Testers may need to ensure a product or process meets specific industry safety standards and therefore does not imperil either the workers involved in the manufacturing process or the end users of the product. They may need to measure emissions from industry sites, or even radiation levels in locations close to nuclear process plants. Customers can therefore range from government departments and pressure groups to pharmaceutical, electronics and manufacturing industries.

It is possible to become an environmental tester by joining a manufacturing company as a general technician and working your way through to that position. Alternatively, you could join a consultancy that specialises in performing environmental tests for clients. For some positions a good scientific academic background is a prerequisite, but it is possible to build up your skills and knowledge from scratch. At the end of the day, the crucial aspects testers need to know are how a product has been put together, or how a process operates and the relevant performance criteria by which measurements should be made.

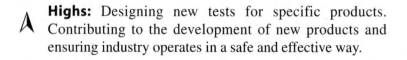

Highs: Designing new tests for specific products. Contributing to the development of new products and ensuring industry operates in a safe and effective way.

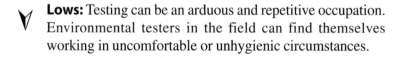

Lows: Testing can be an arduous and repetitive occupation. Environmental testers in the field can find themselves working in uncomfortable or unhygienic circumstances.

Facts, links and trivia

In spite of the perceived hazards and sometimes less than attractive working environment, testing is not a terribly lucrative area of work for the beginner. A trainee working in the area of detecting and managing asbestos may earn as little as £15K. A microbiologist employed to test for impurities in water would be on a similar rate. In the industry, however, these kinds of positions are perceived as the access point for more attractive projects – both financially and in terms of the area of work undertaken.

If you are seeking to make testing your career you should specialise in one area – either linked to a specific product range (electronics, toys, food) – or to certain hazards (radiation, water pollution, stack emissions). More information, including training resources in the field of radiation, can be found at http://www.nrp.org.uk – the Web site for the National Radiological Protection Board – or write to this organisation at National Radiological Protection Board, Chilton, Didcot, Oxon OX11 0RQ. Alternatively two Government sites, the Health and Safety Executive at www.hse.gov.uk and the Department for Environment and Rural Affairs at www.defra.gov.uk/environment/index.htm contain wider information on environmental hazard which must be monitored and managed by law.

Head hunter

For many organisations, the only way to ensure you have the right person for a key job is to go out and find them rather than waiting for them to come to you. Chief executives, finance directors and marketing professionals can find themselves approached by head hunters on a mission to find the right person for a client organisation. In some industries, head hunting is so commonplace it is regarded as the natural way to move from job to job. In IT disciplines, for example, such is the demand for specific programming skills that the only way to identify and attract the required talent is to find ready qualified individuals and make them an offer they can't refuse.

There are various levels of responsibility and functions to be carried out at corporate head hunting offices. To begin with, there is the basic work of finding suitable individuals whose talents match those required by an organisation. When a client first approaches the head hunting company they will have a clear picture of the person they require, what the job will entail and how much they are able to offer that person in terms of remuneration. The vacancy may be for a high-flying 'figurehead' role such as company director or chairman. Alternatively, there could be a very specific set of skills required – a person with specific qualifications, who has certain language skills and is happy to travel around the world carrying out project work, for example.

The head hunter can find the required individual in a variety of ways. For directors or executive appointments, the head hunter may well be able to identify individuals currently in similar roles who would be susceptible to the idea of moving organisations. Potential recruits who are well known within their own industry could be ideal but will only move if the new post involves a rise in status and remuneration. For lower status recruits the head hunter may have to do a bit more rooting around. In the case of finding specific IT programmers, for example, the head hunting agency may employ a number of people to hunt out qualified candidates from existing companies and 'sound out' potential recruits. They will tap into the industry and take recommendations from fellow employees. They will identify the really good performers, those who are leading successful projects and are clearly well motivated.

This part of the job requires very high level communication skills. Most contact is carried out over the phone, with some back up through e-mail, and throughout the process the head hunter must collect crucial information about the candidate, without falsely raising that person's hopes or jeopardising his or her current employment situation by suggesting the move is a certain event.

Initial contact is designed simply to get the individual's CV and to establish whether he or she would be suitable in theory. Having done this, more detailed negotiations can commence. There may be face-to-face interviews between the head hunter and the candidate before the candidate is finally introduced to the client for their own recruitment processes. If all goes well the candidate will then be brought into the client's organisation.

The entire process is conducted in strictest confidence between the hunter and the hunted. On the one hand, the hunter needs to establish the candidate's suitability, while on the other hand the candidate must not burn bridges with their current employer in case things do not work out. As the process moves closer to an offer being made to the candidate, more senior head hunters will become involved in the process. The candidate may have to complete employment suitability tests such as psychometric profiles which give a clear indication of their working and management style.

Head hunting agencies are generally small operations and specialise in recruiting certain staff – whether identified through skills or seniority. It is also the case that many clients in search of new talent will put a number of head hunters on the same job to ensure they get a good selection of candidates.

This practice can bring a good deal of pressure on to the head hunter since in the vast majority of cases the agency is paid on commission only, charging clients a percentage of the successful recruit's initial salary. For this reason it is clearly better for the company to deal with higher status, big earning appointments rather than lower or middle level management. In some cases fees can reach 50 per cent of the candidate's initial year's salary. With such a substantial investment and cost for the client, it is clear the appointment must be successful for the head hunters to stay in business. This method of charging is reflected in remuneration method for employees within head hunting organisations. Even those making initial research and contact will find commission for successful appointments bolsters their basic weekly pay.

 Highs: Finding the right candidate and helping to further both their career and the future of the organisation.

 Lows: Carrying out many interviews with different people and still not securing an appointment. Even when potentially good candidates are found, there may be circumstances beyond your control that prevent the final appointment from going through. Sometimes a candidate is lined up for an interview with the client and then simply does not turn up.

Facts, links and trivia

Head hunters have to be excellent communicators and able to strike up an instant rapport with their quarry if they are to get the information they need. Building a successful relationship with a potential candidate may require an amount of make-believe on the head hunter's part. You may find yourself trying to gain their interest by offering a purely theoretical job, just to get them to send in their CV. You may find yourself suddenly professing to a deep interest in whatever they are interested in, just to establish friendly contact. In one case, a head hunter reported making up a family and kids just so he could share experiences with the candidate with whom he was talking.

Few individuals can be less than flattered when a head hunter considers them to be worth chasing, but this doesn't mean they will instantly take the job. Moreover, the head hunter has to be sure the individual will be successful in his or her new post. It's not enough to just lure someone in through the promise of great riches; you need to be certain the candidate will enjoy the job and be effective for that organisation.

You can find out more about the general area of personnel management through the Chartered Institute of Personnel Directors, 35 Camp Road, Wimbledon SW19 0UX (tel: 020 8971 9000). As the industry's professional body it has up-to-date information, research and training for consultants in this area. For an insight into one specialist head hunting company try Sheffield-Haworth at www.sheffield-haworth.co.uk, 36 Queen Street, London EC4R 1BN.

Rocket builder

The space race is still on. Not only are countries sending probes out into space in order to study our celestial neighbours, but the ever-expanding communications industry means companies are very interested in buying satellites which can receive information from ground level and beam it around the world. In the UK, the Government is funding the Skynet 5 project, a new satellite which will provide the backbone for military communications in the future.

Satellites are designed to orbit the earth at a distance of about 22,000 miles in a geo-stationary orbit, which means they stay fixed over a specific point on the ground. While the industry is relatively small, there are many companies contributing to spacecraft technology. The industry also enjoys a fair amount of crossover with work in the aeroplane industry – indeed, any area that uses high-end technology.

A client may present a company with certain specifications for a satellite such as period of use, position of orbit and accuracy for communicating with stations on the ground. It is up to the design and build team to create that satellite so it can be launched into space on top of a rocket and function perfectly once it has achieved its orbit. The space engineers who do this are generally split between the two functions of structure and propulsion.

Carbon fibre panels are frequently used for the structure, being both light and strong. The satellite must be designed to endure extremes of temperature – sometimes being subject to the full force of the sun on one side and the extreme cold of deep space on the other. Special conductors are fitted to take the heat away from the satellite and ensure the temperature does not rise too high. The craft is propelled and manoeuvred through space by systems that work by squirting hydrazine gas out of nozzles on board the craft. In all aspects of putting the satellite together, there is always a pay-off between features of the technology. One component may be strong but too heavy, another may be light enough but prone to overheating. The designers and engineers need to find the best solution.

The Americans are still engaged in an active manned space programme and in the future space flights could become another option for holiday or leisure time activity. If this is the case there may be the possibility of commercial interest in manned space flight. Commercial interest in turn will bring increased financial resources to the sector, increasing the number of companies involved in this area and therefore opportunities for employment.

Apprenticeships and training schemes are accessible to school-leavers so it is possible to start out as a machine operator and work to achieve a high level of competence and speciality in one area. You should always remember that while technical knowledge is important to the work, being able to operate as part of a team is crucial.

Highs: Space technology is generally recognised as leading many other areas of scientific progress. A breakthrough in this area can contribute to many other areas of scientific endeavour. If you gain specialist skills within the space industry you will be in demand around the world.

Lows: There are only a few companies specialising specifically in space technology. Finding promotion can be difficult simply because there are a limited number of positions within these companies.

Facts, links and trivia

While it is possible to take basic work within a scientific company, without good qualifications you are unlikely to be given a very challenging or satisfying job. Assembling electronic circuitry, you can feel entirely divorced from the idea of getting a rocket into space. Thankfully there are undergraduate and graduate courses in many universities which now focus on the space industry. The Universities of Nottingham, Birmingham, Plymouth and Belfast all run science, astrophysics and aerospace technology-related courses. Even the Open University runs relevant courses in this area.

The best option for aspiring space technicians is to attend an institution that has direct links into commercial organisations who are active in the space industry. This will give you a direct career line into the industry possibly through research projects if not through actual work itself. Surrey Satellite Technology for example (www.sstl.co.uk) has close ties with the University of Surrey.

Mission control manager

According to the British National Space Centre (www.bnsc.gov.uk), the UK is one of the world's biggest users of space data and technology. The civil space industry alone has a workforce of around 6,000 people. While some of these people will work in the technology and building area of the industry, there are many who are responsible for ensuring space flights go according to plan.

Once a satellite has been built, it is up to mission control to see that it achieves its intended geo-stationary orbit above the earth. To do this, flight dynamic technologists and other experts control the satellite once it has blasted off from the launch pad and see that the craft moves into the right position. The flight dynamics team are responsible for the journey the satellite follows. Getting this right is an extremely challenging technical exercise. All sorts of factors need to be considered, including the gravitational pull of the earth on the spacecraft and the timing of the launch so it does arrive at the right point in space at the right time. Other flight specialists will be responsible for the functioning of the satellite – ensuring the deployment of antennae and solar panels is carried out successfully.

Overseeing these teams is the mission control manager. This person is responsible for the success of the entire flight. He or she will give the go-ahead for actions to be taken by members of the control team and if problems occur, it is up to the manager to see each incident is resolved without jeopardising the flight. The manager's job is therefore a people-oriented one – taking a step back from the situation and facilitating the experts to apply their thinking to a problem.

This is not to say mission control managers do not have technical skills – on the contrary, they will have between 10 and 20 years' experience of working with satellites. It is this knowledge that enables them to manage the entire project. They may have started their career working in the flight dynamics area of the business – essentially number crunching work to determine when and where propulsion systems should be used to move the craft into orbit.

Their extensive experience in the business will make them aware of time factors relating to the project and they will know where to look for solutions. The launch mission period itself may last two or three weeks, during which time everyone on the mission control team can expert to be putting in very long hours and to be always on call. However, this is only the tip of the iceberg when it comes to the amount of work they put in for any particular flight. Prior to any mission, the control team will have spent years preparing for the launch, putting procedures into place to launch the craft, undergoing simulation exercises and rehearsing their own actions to address every eventuality. It is only through this extensive preparation work that the team can be confident of a successful flight.

 Highs: Commanding the team that gets the satellite into orbit. Working in a truly ground-breaking area – while the technology may be known, every new project presents new challenges which will inform the rest of the industry.

 Lows: Long and stressful hours during the launch stage. Space missions are extremely expensive and as controller it is your responsibility to ensure all goes well. Some mission control work is relatively mundane number crunching, but it is good to do since it gives you the knowledge of how satellites work.

Facts, links and trivia

As with the rocket builder, the best way into this type of work is through higher education. The British National Space Centre (www.bnsc.gov.uk), 151 Buckingham Palace Road, London SW1W 9SS (tel: 020 7215 0807) has details of courses, career paths and current projects and is important if you want to keep up to date on the space industry in the UK. One of the bidders for the Skynet 5 military satellite project is a consortium made up of BAE SYSTEMS, BT and Lockheed Martin. All three are actively looking for new talent to bring into their organisations and contribute to the future of space technology.

The Space Travel Company is convinced there will be a new market for leisure trips into space with the next 15 years. The company's Web site, www.thespacetravelcompany.co.uk, is the current launch pad for its new enterprise in the travel business. The European Space Agency Web site also carries information on initiatives and vacancies within this organisation and can be found at www.esa.int.

Weather forecaster

There are two types of weather forecaster and consequently two broad paths to achieving the post. The first kind of forecaster is essentially a radio or TV presenter – someone who knows very little about forecasting and meteorology itself but is presentable, enthusiastic and able to read information out clearly. While many of the more established weather services will use qualified forecasters (see below) the rapidly increasing number of media channels could mean it becomes very easy to give weather reports for viewers or listeners without actually knowing anything about why it is raining in the first place.

Qualified weather forecasters are employed in the UK by the Meteorological Office (usually referred to as the Met Office). All the forecasters seen and heard on the BBC come directly from here; however, this is only the tip of the iceberg when it comes to forecasting jobs. The Met Office was established in 1854 to provide information on the wind and sea-currents for mariners and to further the understanding of meteorology. Today, it provides services to the public and to governmental departments including the Department of the Environment, Transport and the Regions and even to the armed forces operating around the world.

Within the Office, employees work under civil servant conditions as forecasters, weather observers, researchers and technical staff. There are also commercial marketing and sales staff whose job it is to push the Office's services to new client areas. Forecasters need to have qualifications in meteorology, but can be employed with high-level science qualifications and receive specific training once they are employed.

The office supplies 3,000 tailored forecasts and briefings to customers every day covering different time periods and geographical areas. 'Nowcasts' cover the weather for the next 6 hours, short range from 6 hours to 3 days, medium range 3–10 days and the monthly prospect covers 10–15 days or 15–30 days. A seasonal forecast predicts conditions 3–6 months ahead while climate predictions offer information projected over the next 10–100 years. This latter forecast is particularly important to organisations such as the DETR and environmental groups who can use the information to help campaign to reduce global warming.

Highs: Interpreting complex data to produce a simple forecast for specific clients.

Lows: Irregular hours and, of course, being blamed for the weather and constantly asked if it will get brighter later.

Facts, links and trivia

The Met Office Web site is at www.met-office.gov.uk, or you can write to them at London Road, Bracknell, Berkshire RG12 2SZ (customer services tel: 0845 3000300). As well as containing up to the minute weather reports, the BBC's site includes weather stories including interviews with some regional and national forecasters. Head for www.bbc.co.uk/weather. Lisa Burke, who presents the weather on Sky, has a Web site www.lisaburke.co.uk which at first appears to highlight the celebrity side of forecasting, but don't be fooled – her autobiography page shows she has had a successful and scientific career in higher education.

The University of East Anglia also train and employ Meteorologists. Its Web page is at www.weatherquest.co.uk or write to University of East Anglia, School of Environmental Sciences, Earlham Road, Norwich NR4 7TJ (tel: 01603 507605).

This is Entertainment

The entertainment world offers both the most diverse range of jobs of any sector and one of the most uncertain job markets. Whether you want to act, direct films, help behind the scenes at concerts and theatres, or work as a children's entertainer, success in the workplace will always be dependent on the current tastes of your audience. This year it might be fine to get a balloon modelling clown for your five-year-old's birthday, but next year you might find nothing but an afternoon of Children's TV stars on video will hold their interest or give them any standing among their peers. Such is the changing face of popular culture.

Added to this, competition for jobs in the sector is fierce with many employees getting work because of who they know rather than what they know. Getting into the industry can mean a long period of knocking on doors and being knocked back. You may find yourself working for very little – possibly no – money in the early days, just to get the opportunity to show what you can do. Even if a level of success is achieved, a sudden change in fashion, negative press coverage or a bad review can lead to disaster and unemployment.

In this section, entertaining people is taken beyond stage, screen and pop music. The leisure industry has grown considerably over the past 10 years. As the pace of modern life has increased and the pressure on workers has gone up, there has been an increased need to get away from it all. Today, everyone may work hard but they really want to party hard as well and so are constantly searching for new and satisfying ways of getting away from it all. The leisure industry is therefore an innovative area, welcoming new ideas which will attract large numbers of customers and large audiences.

Celebrity

For a long time celebrities actually had to be talented in order to make a living. Musicians, singers, actors and even writers could work hard and gain recognition that extended outside their chosen field. They would still continue working in their original field, but celebrity status would give them increased opportunities to extend their work, appearing on chat shows, panel games and so on. Today, however, it is more than possible to become a celebrity while having very little talent at all. All you need to do is to be in the right place at the right time.

Over the past few years the rise of 'reality TV programmes' has provided a great way of becoming famous for just being yourself. This started with the 'docu-soap' – a new programme format that took the premise of a documentary structure, but then followed specific storylines and characters in order to keep the viewer's interest rather than telling one single story. One of the early programmes, for example, centred on the people and activities of a driving school. Among the storylines was a woman who was destined never to pass her test. In spite of her ineptitude she became a household name for a while, appearing on *This Is Your Life* and recording a pop song.

At one point you couldn't move in the evening TV schedules without bumping up against another docu-soap, complete with its colourful character – be it an airline assistant, traffic warden or local London resident. Then another level of reality TV appeared. This time, rather than going out and finding a situation which would make good television, the programme makers created their own situations where real people could play off each other. In *Big Brother*, a number of ordinary people were locked up together and 'competed' to be the last person left in the house. This was followed by similar formats involving people being forced to stay together, including one where participants were chained by the ankle to each other to see what would happen. Finally there came the competition programmes where ordinary members of the public were given the chance to compete to become a pop star, soap star or fashion model.

As each new format has been repeated and reworked, the likelihood of those featured to become celebrities has declined. The first *Big Brother* programme resulted in three or four contestants securing agents, future TV work and book deals. Second time around, there hasn't been as much interest.

The trick of becoming a celebrity is to stir the interest of the public – to capture their imagination, provoke, shock or annoy; to offer them a personality or a story which they just can't get enough of and to this extent you certainly don't need to be a contestant in a TV show. If you have a good story, there's nothing to stop you from getting in touch with the press or a good PR agency and getting them to handle your exposure from there. Hanging out with other celebrities – no matter how low down on the fame scale they may be – will certainly get you noticed and if you play your cards right there's plenty of money to be had through telling your story or giving your opinions on any given subject the press are interested in.

Naturally, there is a harder way to achieve celebrity and that is through hard work and determination in your specific field. The pop, film, TV and art industries are still on the look-out for hot new property. But you'll never get true celebrity status without selling a good image of yourself that people want to buy in to. Think of the sudden trend in British Gangster movies inspired by Guy Richie's film *Lock Stock and Two Smoking Barrels*. Alternatively, think of the incredible popularity of the 'late 20-something' female novel or of the fashion scene and press coverage which has grown up around the club scene. In each case, a real trend has appeared because sufficient numbers of people want to identify with those forms of entertainment. It is still often the case that talent is recognised if the individual sticks at their work for long enough, but true popularity will only happen when the image which goes along with what you do appeals to the masses.

 Highs: Parties, high life, other celebrities and a generally hedonistic lifestyle.

 Lows: Many celebrities suffer depression and break-downs. Being dependent on public opinion means you are always at risk when public opinion turns against you.

Facts, links and trivia

Keep up to date with upcoming TV shows that could be looking for your talent or personality by checking out the industry press Broadcast – subscriptions via Tower House, Sovereign Park, Market Harborough, Leicestershire LE16 9EF, e-mail: BRO@subscription.co.uk (tel: 01858 438847) or Web site www.produxion.com.

There are also Web sites where you can create your own home page specifically to sell your creative talents to producers and broadcasters. Check out www.neverheardofthem.co.uk for starters.

Finally, a number of stars found their fame through carrying out menial jobs such as research positions in TV companies and tape operators for record companies. Trawl through any media directory to find employers who might give you a break in this area – *The Knowledge* (United Business Media Information Services) is probably the most comprehensive and should be found at most good libraries (it's far too expensive to buy yourself).

Cinema projectionist

The cinema projectionist is the last but also perhaps one of the most important people in the success of a film. It's not simply that without a projectionist the audience would not see the film, but frequently projectionists are responsible for the entire experience of going to the movies. They control all the sound and light systems within cinema auditoriums, so once seated the audience is entirely in their hands.

Before the show has even started the projectionist needs to make sure the auditorium is a pleasant and safe place for members of the public to come to. They are responsible for the heating and ventilation of the room and ensuring there is appropriate and functional safety equipment on hand.

Cinemas operate to very strict timings. They will arrange a certain number of screenings throughout the day based on the length of the film and how popular they believe it will be with the public. Very often one screening will finish with only 10 or 15 minutes to spare before the audience for the next show are allowed into the auditorium. In order to ensure the right number of screenings is made, the projectionist must make each showing start at the right time. There is no opportunity to allow latecomers to be admitted and comfortably seated; the programme must start as advertised.

The projectionist will dim the house lights at the right time – and the right speed – at the start of each programme and operate the curtain in front of the screen where fitted. A true professional will make sure the projected picture does not hit the screen until the curtain has been completely drawn.

Projecting the show itself means showing adverts and trailers for future films as well as the feature presentation the audience has paid to see. Film projectionists may pause projection between trailers and the presentation, according to the procedures used within the cinema. Some cinemas pause between the two parts of the programme to allow latecomers to get themselves settled while others still use this opportunity to send in ushers with refreshments. In both cases it is up to the projectionist to make sure the break runs smoothly and to time.

Developments in projection room technology means that reel-to-reel changeovers during long movies have been replaced, but new equipment still requires skilled operation and training is extremely important. Sound equipment is also complex and many auditoriums use a series of speakers to give full surround sound. Mixing this sound from the projection room can be an art in itself.

Clearly film projectionists must also be prepared to work unsociable hours and be ready to work alone from the projection room. If problems occur, as a projectionist you need to be technically minded enough to fix them and maintain the smooth running of the evening. You may like films very much – and indeed, you should have some interest in the industry to work as a projectionist – but remember, all the time you are working from the projection room you are not sitting in the auditorium. This means you are likely to see the same film over and over again.

 Highs: There is a genuine sense of satisfaction to be had from watching the response of an audience to a film.

 Lows: There could be times when you play an unpopular film repeatedly to a half empty auditorium.

Facts, links and trivia

It is now possible to gain an NVQ in cinema projection, demonstrating competence in the discipline which can be recognised throughout the industry. Many multiplex cinemas such as

Odeon or Warner Brothers run their own training programmes for projectionists, according to the equipment they use and the procedures they expect to be followed at each venue.

The British Kinematograph Sound and Television Society (www.bksts.com) was founded in 1931 and now promotes and supports film industry workers. Meanwhile, the British Federation of Film Societies links together the many and diverse film societies across the UK. This organisation will put you in touch with local resources to help you develop your interest. Its Web site is at www.bffs.co.uk or you can write to The Ritz Building, Mount Pleasant Campus, Swansea Institute of Higher Education, Swansea SA1 6ED (tel: 01792 481170).

Pyrotechnics specialist

There are two kinds of pyrotechnics specialist. There are those who manage outdoor displays – huge public spectacles for November 5th, New Year and special events – and those who work on indoor effects. The latter cover all theatrical effects – from the genie who appears in a puff of smoke to the huge explosions that are a necessary part of any action adventure feature film. There is some crossover between these two areas – and often the two disciplines use similar equipment – but in general a pyrotechnics company will do better marketing to one or the other of these areas rather than both.

Of course, working with explosives means taking a great deal more care than simply not returning to a firework once it has been lit. Training is available – there's even a BTEC qualification for Firers at Loughborough College – but in general you'll get training on the job. Once in a company you'll find out about the different products, the effects they have and how to use them safely.

Being a successful pyrotechnic operator is a great technical challenge. In many cases – and especially with outdoor events – you will have only one chance to get it right. A celebratory event may be leading up to a massive fireworks display, perhaps coordinated to music. Prior to the event, the pyrotechnic operators will consider the display from start to finish – when certain flares, rockets and explosions should take place, how they can be coordinated, whether they should be set to music and so on. A truly effective display is not one where everything goes up at once, but where specific effects are chosen and placed to go off in a synchronised way.

Pyrotechnics in the theatre and film also have to operate correctly and safely on cue. The effect might be used in the vicinity of actors and it is the responsibility of the pyrotechnic operator to ensure that no-one is hurt. In film, it may be possible to rearrange stunt explosions, but to do so incurs incredible cost to the film producers. Once again, it's a job where everything should happen right first time and the only way to ensure this is through preparation and experience.

Outdoor pyrotechnics companies will get most of their work between November 5th and the New Year. The work is therefore seasonal, although some large companies employ as many as 100 operators year round to meet demand for parties and special events on a nationwide basis. It is certainly an area where you should join an established company to learn the ropes rather than trying to set out on your own. This is not just because you need to learn your craft from people already in the industry, but because of cost. Pyrotechnic companies need large cash flows to be able to carry the stock they need, and also must be fully insured against the occurrence of any accident.

Highs: Working in a team to prepare and create an astonishing display.

Lows: Working outdoors during the winter months means being cold and wet for a lot of the time. Just remember the display itself is the tip of the iceberg of the work.

Facts, links and trivia

The BTEC qualification is at Loughborough College, Radmoor Road, Loughborough, Leicestershire LE11 3BT (tel: 01509 215831) www.loucoll.ac.uk and is the only qualification to be recognised by the Pyrotechnic Sub-Group of the Explosive Industry Group of the CBI (www.eig.org.uk) or Explosives Industry Group, CBI, Centrepoint, 103 New Oxford Street, London WC1A 1DU. This forum works alongside the Health and Safety Executive and DTI creating policy and overseeing legislation and training for the pyrotechnics industry.

The fireworks safety site of the British Pyrotechnics Association is at www.fireworks.co.uk and contains a link to one of the few online journals for the industry. Alternatively, you can write to the Association care of: KPMG, 1 Waterloo Way, Leicester LE1 6LP.

The annual British Fireworks Championship was held in Plymouth last year at the beginning of August (in spite of the fact that the long days meant blast-off couldn't start until 10 pm). Since most fireworks are manufactured overseas, British companies are judged on criteria such as rhythm, continuity and overall spectacle created – rather than how good a particular firework actually is.

Jingle writer

Getting your songs recorded and heard can be an uphill struggle. Making money out of your music is even more difficult. You may have dreams of pop stardom, or of writing a fantastic movie score, but achieving those dreams may be frustrating and more than a little draining on your bank account. While waiting for the big breakthrough to arrive, musicians can make a handsome living out of jingle writing – putting together short catchy tunes that promote products and companies on the radio and even on the television. Jingle writing not only allows you to use your talents and get your music heard, but can pay handsomely while leaving you with sufficient time to follow your own musical dreams.

Jingle writing pays so well because real skill is needed to do it effectively. When clients approach a writer with a brief, they may have very clear ideas of what they want. They may already have a 'tag line' – a phrase which represents their company and product succinctly – that they want incorporated into the jingle. They may have a clear idea of the style and feel of the jingle – whether it should be jokey and fun or serious and sober. They might have a musical style in mind. Alternatively, the client may have little idea of what they want. The nightmare job occurs when a client doesn't know what they want until they hear it. The writer may then find him- or herself reworking the piece again and again. Not only is this frustrating for the writer, but also, with a deadline looming, the client will not be happy either.

The jingle writer must be able to incorporate all the client's requirements into the jingle and do so within a specific time-frame – usually no more than 30 seconds. The jingle can only be this length in order to meet the requirements of the broadcasting company. Longer jingles cost more to broadcast as well as more money to make.

Jingle writing is a specialist field of advertising work and some writers may well start their careers in large advertising companies. Occasionally writers will be linked to media broadcast companies, especially radio stations, who will provide a service to clients who would like to advertise on the radio but do not have the production experience or contacts to create their own jingles. The jingle writer may also find they are given work to create 'idents' – jingles which promote the station and specific shows.

Many jingle writers get away from the 9 to 5 slog, however, and by going freelance can manage their own time, working on their own projects alongside commissioned work. This is really only possible when the jingle writer has built a good reputation and has a number of reliable contacts who will offer work. The writer may also find work in creating incidental music for TV or radio shows, gradually expanding his or her repertoire as time goes by.

 Highs: Creating a piece of music that expresses precisely and efficiently what the client wants to say about the product.

 Lows: Constant rewriting when clients aren't sure what they want. If you are working within an advertising agency you will be under pressure to complete this task and move on to the next project. If you are freelancing, the situation could be more serious since you are only paid on delivery.

Facts, tips and links

Many jingle writers are solo workers. However, as a jingle writer you must have a good network of contacts and friends to support you. While work usually comes from advertising agencies and sometimes directly from clients, you may find more work through contacts with a local recording studio. Jingle writing is an advertising job rather than a purely music related exercise. You may receive some praise for your technical use of music but you will only have success and be recommissioned if your jingle actually sells the product it features. Pay will relate to the size of the project and clients you are writing for. A simple orchestrated tune with single vocal may net up to £500 a time, but a nationwide ad campaign will bring you thousands. Big earners have produced tunes for national TV contracts such as TV channel idents or theme tunes. Every time these are played, the jingle writer receives royalty payments.

There are many sites where jingles can be downloaded from the Internet. Freespace.virgin.net/radio.jingles is soon to deliver a range of MP3 files while www2.prestel.co.uk/page42/whba_jingles2.htm strangely offers a selection of ditties from Wycombe Radio. There's a comprehensive site created by an ex-DJ who clearly became obsessed with the subject at radiojinglesonline.users.btopenworld.com – the site includes links to jingle companies as well as samples from around the world.

Scenery painter

Scenic artists do not simply create art to look nice; they work to create entire environments in which performances can take place. Scenery painters work on sets which appear in theatres, on film, television and even in magazine articles. They might work to create locations from a specific time period or place, or produce more abstract, atmospheric locations which provide a backdrop for a performance. While scenery painters obviously work on a larger scale than many artists, the techniques and processes they use are similar.

Working on a stage set is a collaborative process. The creation of the set will have begun with the set designer meeting the director of the play or film to discuss requirements and the overall artistic objectives of the performance. There will be a strict timetable by which time the set must be completed and a clear budget to control costs. Using either a scale model of the proposed set or computer-aided design, the designer will arrive at what the set should look like.

The set designer will then bring in an array of skilled workers to realise the set. In theatre and films set builders will be employed to build platforms, walls, doors and windows. These will be basic but functional constructions and it is up to the scenery painters to ensure they look real and convincing for the audience. While scenery painters will be skilled artists in their own right, they must work to realise the designer's vision.

Sometimes set painters will use domestic materials to create a realistic feel to a set. They might select appropriate wallpaper or paint for a room. At the same time there are special decorating techniques for stage and film use. Often sets require a 'lived in' look – the appearance of dirt and grim from years of use. Props and scenery can be 'broken down' in such a way as to give the impression that they are old and neglected. The scenery painter may also need to treat shiny or reflective surfaces on the set to prevent them from dazzling the camera, audience or actors when the lights are on.

In spite of working on such a grand scale, some of the scenery painter's work is detailed and delicate. The painter may have to create a backdrop to give the impression of a view through a window which stands up to scrutiny whether viewed from the rear of the theatre or from the front row. Details such as shadows and even entire pictures may be painted onto scenery walls rather than hanging an actual picture there.

The scenery painter must have an extensive knowledge of paints and decorating materials. The texture and finish of paint will have a huge impact on the way the final set looks when film or theatre lights are rigged up around it. Colours can change under these lights and will certainly look different from normal daylight conditions. At the same time safety is an important consideration. There are many flammable materials used in set building and the set painter must ensure they are handled and applied in a safe manner.

Scenery painters may work for individual companies such as theatres, studios or dedicated scenery manufacturers. As a newcomer to the industry you should find yourself an apprentice-like position in such a company and learn alongside those who have been doing the job for a while. As your expertise increases you may be able to work on a freelance basis, switching between projects and even from theatre to TV or film and back as the work arises.

 Highs: Creating a special effect which complements and works with the overall production using limited materials.

 Lows: Long hours and a high level of pressure to meet production deadlines.

Facts, links and trivia

BECTU is the Broadcasting, Entertainment, Cinematography and Theatre Union based at 111 Wardour Street, London W1V 4AY (tel: 020 7437 8506). It has regional divisions and represents the interests of diverse creative artists and craftspeople across the industry. Its Web site at www.bectu.org.uk carries news and an extensive portal to training and industry resources. A European Web site with contributions from staff at the Royal National Theatre includes input from a scenery artist and can be found via www.acquis.org.uk.

To get some idea of other areas of set construction, take a look at www.studiopark.co.uk. This company has been running for over 25 years designing and creating stage sets on a massive scale including stages for tours by the Rolling Stones and Pink Floyd as well as corporate and national events such as the launch of the Sony PS2 and the Commonwealth Games Manchester 2002.

Puppeteer

Puppetry means more than Punch and Judy. Today's puppet-based performances are frequently the most innovative and affecting pieces of theatre around. Identified for the main part with children's theatre, there are also adult puppet theatre companies offering intriguing and imaginative pieces of work. There is an international audience for this work and regular puppet festivals are held all over the world. Puppets also play a large part in street theatre and carnivals, with puppeteers building and operating huge marionettes that tower above their audiences. Puppeteers can work on both the small and big screen, not simply with kids' programmes such as *Sesame Street* or Saturday morning children's programmes, but also for creating leading characters such as monsters or aliens for blockbuster movies.

It is not necessary to have had a theatrical background to work with puppets. You may have an interest in textiles or craft activities. Whatever the case you will need a good imagination and sufficient practical skills to design and assemble your own creations. Puppets can be made using a wide range of materials from wood and cloth through to rubber latex or simply paper silhouettes. As with all performance-related work, the most likely way into this area is through voluntary work and proving your worth through making your own creations. Puppeteers must be able to work with other people, understanding the design and concept of the performance or show that the puppets will be used for. They must be able to work to deadlines creating their puppets and have a good level of physical coordination to be able to operate the puppets successfully.

Puppets have also been used for educational purposes – one puppeteer found herself working for the local leisure centre creating floating puppets which would teach children about safety in water. Puppets have also been used therapeutically when working with children who have suffered trauma. The children found it easier to talk about their experiences using the puppets rather than relating their stories directly.

In recent years the use of computer imaging and animatronics has taken puppetry into a new area. TV programmes such as *Walking with Dinosaurs* have required puppeteers to build and operate complex technology to tell the story of animals which died out many years ago. While animatronics technology may be a long way from the common perception of glove puppets, the techniques required for operating them and telling stories using them is the same.

 Highs: Creating new characters and shows.

 Lows: Work can be erratic, pay is not always good and puppeteers may find themselves taking on uninspiring projects in order to pay the rent.

Facts, links and trivia

Punch and Judy were originally marionette puppets – they were operated through using strings from above, rather than from below as today's puppets are. A history of Punch and puppetry can be found at www.users.breathemail.net/punchjames/punch-history.htm. Some film directors have found puppetry techniques useful from a cost and logistics point of view – one successful film director started out with a film in which the only characters featured were Barbie dolls.

The Puppet Centre offers resources, information and useful links and is based at BAC, Lavender Hill, London SW11 5TN (tel: 020 7228 5335) www.puppetcentre.com. The Little Angel Theatre is a small venue in London creating performances principally for children. It's located at Dagmar Terrace, London N1 2BN (tel: 020 7226 1787) www.littleangeltheatre.com.

Circus performer

The circus used to be purely a family business. The skills, show-manship and even the big top would stay in the family, handed down from generation to generation. This is no longer the case. Firstly, the circus has moved away from being a trained animal spectacle to being a people-oriented show of skills. From the Chinese and Russian State Circuses, to Circus Oz and the work of Archaos and the Circus of Horrors, this form of entertainment has been redefined, bringing in new talent and creating new shows.

The idea behind Archaos and the Circus of Horrors was to use the traditional circus structure – the big top and the show-manship – but to inject it with a contemporary anarchic element – punk rock and horror show styles. There would still be clowns and jugglers, but now they would chase one another with chain saws and juggle fish while riding motorbikes. Sure there would be a trapeze act, but the trapeze would be suspended from an industrial crane. In short, animals were taken out of the equation and imagination was brought in.

Companies such as Cirque du Soleil and Cirque Eloize have taken up the baton and toured the world with theatre-based shows. In this instance, circus skills have been applied to a more emotion-driven narrative – the rope gymnast performs to express his or her love, the clowns are jealous of each other and so on.

Circus skills are used in many other areas of the entertainment industry. They are great for street entertainment and unicyclists and jugglers are always to be found at Covent Garden in London or whenever there is a suitable festival in the UK. Performers can also find work on TV and the stage when performances require their special skills. Circus performers may also be employed in the business world as part of corporate events – spectacular launch parties or other celebratory events.

Obviously this is all physically demanding stuff. You do not need to be in prime condition and able to juggle right now – you can learn these skills with determination and enthusiasm – but you will need a lot of stamina. Even at the peak of your skills, you may find it hard to cope with this demanding work day after day, preparing for a show, maybe even putting up the big top, and sleeping in basic mobile accommodation.

Getting these skills has become relatively easy. There are no end of workshops teaching you how to juggle or do the diablo. There are even sessions which will teach high wire and trapeze acts or clowning techniques. Once you have learnt the basics, you can then experiment with your skills and extend your performance repertoire. You will find imagination and originality are treasured in this field. And once you have established yourself as a competent performer you will be able to make money through running your own classes and passing the skills on to the next generation.

 Highs: Challenging yourself to new physical achievements while entertaining people with something they cannot do.

 Lows: Work can be erratic and audiences vary.

Facts, links and trivia

Circus courses are run all around the country at arts centres and colleges. The Circus Space, Coronet Street, London N1 6HD, www.thecircusspace.co.uk (tel: 020 7613 4141) runs a wide variety of courses, usually beginning with a taster session so students can find the discipline they prefer. A dedicated circus school has also been established in Belfast at 23–5 Gordon Street, Belfast BT1 2LG, www.belfastcircus.org (tel: 028 9023 6007). The Kent Circus School is at 58 St Anne's Road, Tankerton, Whitstable, Kent (tel: 01227 264907).

There's a useful batch of links at www.skylight-circus-arts.org.uk/othersites.html; and Tom Tom Troupe, offering circus supplies amongst other information, can be found at www.myjugglingsite.fsnet.co.uk or Unit 8, Clevedon House, Prince of Wales Road, Cromer, Norfolk NR27 9HR.

Montage/demontage crew

A classic summer job, montage staff are employed to travel around foreign campsites putting up tents (montage) at the beginning of the summer season and taking them down (demontage) at the end of the season. A doddle. And even better than that, a doddle you can almost treat as a fully paid holiday.

The reason this job exists is that some holidaymakers like the idea of camping in Europe, but either do not have their own tent or cannot face the idea of putting it up themselves. Instead, a holiday company will book a ready-erected tent for them and kit it out with as many mod cons as possible – a fridge, a cooker, beds, etc. All the holidaymakers need to do is drive to their holiday site and take up residency in their very own ready-made tent. Before the season begins, therefore, the holiday companies must find a bunch of people who will go and put up the tents, plug in all the necessary appliances and ensure the sites are ready for the holidaymakers.

It can be hard and tiring work. The tents will have been in storage over the winter together with all the other equipment, resulting in bent poles, damaged canvases and mouldy fridges. Pitching the tents is only part of the process. All the equipment must be cleaned, sorted and replaced if there is anything missing. However, it can be a very enjoyable way to spend a few weeks or months – as long as the weather is good and you find yourself working with a nice bunch of fellow montage workers.

If you are lucky and want to stay for the entire season you may be able to get work as a site host or a crèche attendant. This way, once you have put all the tents up you will be left on a campsite ready for the first holiday arrivals. Site hosts are not simply there to ensure the holidaymakers have a good time, but since the sites are loaned from the owner of the campsite they may need to liaise with the owner as well. In such cases it can be useful to have foreign language skills.

Highs: Working abroad, travelling and meeting people.

 Lows: Can be hard manual labour and you must be prepared to put up tents in all weather and to a strict deadline.

Facts, links and trivia

Montage and other seasonal staff are recruited between October and April each year. The main two companies offering these kinds of breaks are Eurosites www.eurosites.co.uk (tel: 01254 300622) which is part of the Airtours Group of companies, and Eurocamp www.eurocamp.co.uk based at Hartford Manor, Greenbank Lane, Northwich, Cheshire CW8 1HW (tel: 01606 787000). The latter company is part of Holidaybreak plc who now runs a useful jobsite at www.holidaybreakjobs.com offering access to jobs abroad and in the UK.

If you fancy checking out the latest in the range of tents manufactured or any other information about camping, caravanning and other outdoor pursuits, head for www.oakwood-village.com.

Karaoke party host

Coming live to a venue near you, the karaoke party is a chance for everyone to get up and strut their stuff, taking their dreams of pop stardom one stage further than standing in front of their bedroom mirror with a hairbrush. The basic format is this: karaoke host turns up at party venue – or even just a room in a pub – bringing a public address (PA) system, a TV screen or two and a number of laser or digital disks which will play the backing tracks and the words to each tune on the TV screen.

People at the party or in the pub select a song they would like to have a go at, take the microphone and sing along to the tune following the words displayed on the TV screen. As a result, everyone falls about laughing because the singers are so awful or they spend the rest of the night being very quiet and occasionally saying, 'They should be professional singers, you know'.

If you do not have the picture yet, being a karaoke host requires an enormous amount of self-confidence (some might say lack of self-consciousness). As host it is up to you to raise the party spirit, inspire the crowd and encourage people to get up on stage and perform. This task can vary from being like trying to get blood from a stone to a matter of crowd control – depending on how forthcoming the audience is. You will have to do the first song yourself to show how it is done – or possibly the first hour if the audience proves reluctant – or even the entire night if it does not go very well. You do not need to have professional training but as the host you should not really go anywhere near the equipment without an average singing voice and an extrovert personality. Bear in mind also that if you are going to sing night after night, your business will soon go to pot if you lose your voice.

A bit of market research around pubs, clubs and private parties will put you in the picture as to how many shows you could expect to do every month and you may find enough regular engagements to justify the large investment in your own equipment.

Alternatively, there are entertainment agencies who offer such shows and you may do better tracking one of these down and seeking employment with them. In London, there is now a club specifically devoted to karaoke. Private rooms equipped with their own machines can be booked by groups of people, allowing them to sing badly at each other without distressing other members of the public.

 Highs: Meeting people and putting on a show.

 Lows: Having to endure another dreadful version of Robbie Williams' 'Angels'.

Facts, links and trivia

A basic karaoke set up including enough tracks to start up costs around £400. However, you'll need a few other gizmos to make the party really swing – lighting effects, additional microphones and so on. www.karaoke-discs.com offers information on equipment.

There are four karaoke formats, each offering different benefits in terms of how much of a multimedia experience you want to provide and how many tracks can be stored on a single disk. Laserdisc and CD graphics (CDG) were the first formats, usually supporting a blue screen with the words coming up in time with the music. VCD and DVD (video CD and digital video disc) offer background videos as well as the words. There are currently around 56,000 songs recorded on the CDG format, compared to only 8,000 on VCD and 5,000 on DVD. That said, the most popular songs for your audience will feature in all formats, simply because the manufacturers usually select only those which have charted in the UK or the United States.

TV/film extra

Also known as 'background artists' these are the people you see hanging around the pub on TV while the leading actor argues with the barman. They just happen to be passing when the hero of the film is running down the street – glimpsed for a moment and then gone forever. In spite of this brevity, being an extra is still a skilled job and workers will need some level of training as well as being members of the actors' union Equity. It is not very easy to act naturally and background artists may need to repeat precise actions over and over again for the needs of shooting.

Getting yourself into the frame is usually a matter of word of mouth and keeping your eyes peeled for useful advertisements. Papers like *The Stage* carry notifications of auditions but approach with extreme caution the agency adverts that offer to register you for extras' work for a fee. In recent years, many of these operations have proved to be scams with the so-called agency taking fees from people and not doing anything to get them work.

Being an extra can be far removed from the bright lights of Hollywood. Extras may find themselves hanging around for long periods of time doing nothing while the film crew set up a shot and try to get the material they want. There is the chance that you will be selected for a particular role as an extra – you may have to interact with the lead characters or you may be a definite character who stands out from the crowd. If you are identifiable in one shot you may find you are released from the rest of the day's shooting – the next shot could be ruined if you appear to be in two places at once.

It is imperative that you are well behaved on set and do exactly what you are told. It is not simply a question of getting the camera shot right; there is often very heavy equipment or scaffolding in use on a film set that can be dangerous. Budding actors should beware of doing too much extra work. It should not be viewed as a path to landing major roles and inevitably could be limiting for your career if producers and casting directors perceive you only as background cast.

 Highs: Appearing on screen and being part of the making of a film.

 Lows: A lot of waiting around for a very short appearance in a production.

Facts, links and trivia

Extras and background artists can make between £70 and £200 per day. There may be additional money on offer for night shoots, if you have special skills, or a certain look that the film company has been specifically tracking down. The Stage and Television Today is at 47 Bermondsey Street, London SE1 3XT, (tel: 020 7403 1818) and it has a Web site at www.thestage.co.uk. The actor's union Equity, at Guild House, Upper St Martin's Lane, London WC2H 9EG (tel: 020 7379 6000) www.equity.org.uk will give advice and guidance for those who want to work in this area and every acting school offers part- and full-time courses to develop skills.

There are many Web sites offering contacts for extra work, but again, treat them all with caution. There is also a useful free database service for actors' CVs at www.actornet.co.uk, PO Box 5933, Hall Green, Birmingham B28 0XF. If you want to see an example of what happens when film extra work goes wrong, track down the BBC film of Jack Rosenthal's play *Ready When You Are Mr McGill*.

Club promoter/DJ

What to do on a Saturday night is now a complex question. The proliferation of new club nights and dance music genres has blown this area of the nightlife industry wide open. Moreover, in the UK's larger cities it has become a seven-days-a-week business with clubs opening every night playing the music the clubbers want to hear. The fact is, anyone can set up his or her own club night on some scale. If the music is right and the crowds enjoy the evening, there is no limit to how far the club night can go – successful promoters and DJs even produce their own merchandise to go with the club such as clothing and compilation records of music.

However, creating your own club and ensuring it is full of enthusiastic revellers is a time-consuming and exhausting affair. First you have to find a venue. You may be able to talk a club or café into giving you an evening (usually a quiet evening) on which to try your hand, but it could mean hiring the upstairs function room in a local pub. You need to have a clear idea of what the night is going to consist of – what kind of people you want to attract, what music will be played and so on. All this will affect the way you put the night together, the image of the club and the promotional work you need to do to get people there.

Alongside the hard work, however, putting a club night together can be extremely good fun and enables you to work with lots of different people on one project. There may be visual artists you can use to provide wall hangings, video and film artists who can create projections to accompany the music and lighting designers who will help to generate the right atmosphere in the venue. You may have a good enough record collection and enough experience to DJ yourself, but you should have guest DJs from time to time who will provide different music and could be an additional draw for the crowd. This could mean finding the finance to pay those DJs – finance which inevitably comes from the people who walk through the door.

You are going to need a fair amount of money up front to set up your club. Venue hire, sound and light hire need funding and even the DJs will want paying before you have started to count up the cash at the front door. Ensuring that you do not lose money on the event means you need to set door prices that will cover your expenses when you get a certain number of clubbers in. Get more numbers than that and you start making money. If you are successful in one venue you can offer the night to other places and begin to negotiate better terms for yourself. As you play in bigger venues the door takings will rise while your operating costs stay basically the same.

 Highs: You create a place that you enjoy and others do too.

 Lows: Arranging everything – it is best to do this in a team and make sure everyone pulls their weight.

Facts, links and trivia

In order to be successful you must find yourself an excellent supply of records. This means finding a well-connected shop which can get hold of the latest releases as soon as possible. You'll know you're successful when you start to receive records direct from the artists and record companies before they hit the shelves – at this point the record companies will expect you to promote their artists by playing their records during your set. Web links can be used to find new and obscure recordings. www.juno.co.uk is an excellent dance music resource updated weekly with news of releases and access to MP3 files to preview tracks. www.htfr.com is the Web site offshoot of Hard To Find Records based at 10 Upper Gough Street, Birmingham. The site deals with playing equipment as well as the records you want to play.

Setting up your own DJ system will be expensive, as you need high quality equipment. Decks could cost as much as £400, mixers around £300 and headphones £100.

While you can build your career for yourself, you may eventually want to find an agent or management company to take care of bookings and administration. To get an idea of the kind of people currently making it big on the club circuit, check out the Web site of the agency Unlimited DJs at www.djindex.com (based at 93 Otterfield Road, Yewsley, West Drayton, Middlesex UB7 8PF).

Location manager

This job is one of the more high-pressured roles within TV but can be rewarding both financially and personally. Location managers are attached to specific TV programmes to find suitable locations where they can be recorded. A single episode of a drama, for example, could mean a list of requirements covering several different interior and exterior locations. The location manager must go out and find places which match these requirements, making sure the owners or residents are willing to let their lives be disrupted by a few days of filming.

Even when a film or TV programme is set at a foreign location, the chances are that the shoot will eventually happen in the UK. Indeed, it's more than likely that the location will be found not too far away from London. This is partly due to logistics: most of the TV production industry operates out of London so getting all the necessary resources – everything from actors' green room facilities to lighting rigs – needs to be kept as simple and as inexpensive as possible.

Once a location has been found, the location manager's job is still not done. When filming takes place the manager is respon-sible for every aspect of the location, from ensuring the production vehicles have space to park to cleaning up the mess left by the film crew at the end of each day. Location managers need to anticipate problems which may arise during the shoot and deal with them to ensure filming runs smoothly. They may need to inform the local police that filming is taking place, ask the locals to keep the noise down during recording or deal with spectators who are naturally drawn by the appearance of a film crew.

Dealing with all these elements can make location management a nightmare of a job, but it also has its rewards. The manager gets to meet lots of interesting people both in and outside the TV industry and can make a clear and strong contribution to the look and feel of a show. The manager is involved at the heart of producing the finished show.

No one would get a job in location management as soon as he or she enters the TV profession – it is a role that requires an appreciation of the whole production process. Some may become location managers after working their way through the production ranks, beginning as a runner, for example, who literally runs around the film unit carrying out different jobs as required.

 Highs: A vital role in TV and film, the location manager has a great contribution to make to television programmes and can work across a variety of projects.

 Lows: Long hours and very stressful work.

Facts, links and trivia

The quickest route to this work is through a Skillset supported training course. Skillset is the Sector Skills Council for the industry and can be contacted at 2nd Floor, 103 Dean Street, London W1D 3TH (tel: 020 7534 5300) and www.skillset.org. A particularly popular course is run by FT2 – Film and Television Freelance Training, 4th Floor, Warwick House, 9 Warwick Street, London W1R 5RA (tel: 020 7734 5141) www.ft2.org.uk.

Work and information may also be tracked down via the Film Council – www.filmcouncil.org.uk, 10 Little Portland Street, London W1W 7JG (tel: 020 7861 7861). As members of the public become more aware of the potential revenue they can realise from hiring their homes and property out to production companies, the location manager's work is likely to become even harder as locations must still be found for the amount available in the programme's budget.

Performance artist

The term performance artist is usually applied to performers whose work does not seem to fit in any single category – theatre, dance or visual arts. These performers will sometimes perform in a conventional theatre space but could essentially stage an event wherever they feel inclined – be it an art gallery, a public space or a car park. Similarly, they may not restrict themselves to one single mode of expression. A single show could comprise music, song, dance and visual art. But how is it possible to make money through this kind of performance?

To begin with, there are a number of festivals, national and international, where new work is commissioned from artists. These may be dedicated art festivals or more general festivities based around a geographic location or a calendar event. Artists may find they are able to suggest, create and perform unique shows which bring something special to the event. One group of performance artists, for example, specialise in a show in which they dress in silver tubes, moving and intersecting with one another to the delight of audiences. They are a particular hit with the public at street festivals. Another troop known as 'The Cone Heads' (who do have pointy heads) interact and improvise with festival crowds, causing curiosity and laughter.

Artists can find work in unlikely places. Private companies sometimes employ artists and writers to work with their customers and employees to bring something different to their everyday business. Poets and writers in residence, for example, offer activities which put a different spin on working the day-to-day grind, while on-site entertainment can help raise morale.

Finding out where these opportunities exist is a question of getting yourself involved in the artistic world. There are a number of useful newsgroups and mailing lists on the Internet where performers share information about upcoming bursaries and festivals. Alternatively, getting yourself involved in a performance group will provide you with first-hand knowledge of where to look for funding. Being a successful artist is never going to mean lots of money but by applying your talent to many different circumstances – from festivals to workplaces – it is possible to do what you want to do without starving.

 Highs: Turning in a good performance and finding new performance areas.

Lows: Poverty.

Facts, links and trivia

There are also performance artists who are so called because they paint or draw pictures of performances – ie a sketch or painting of an actor or ballerina on stage. Once an artist gets a reputation for this line of work single portraits can sell for £500 or more depending on the artist depicted and the popularity of the artist.

Meanwhile, funding, festivals and performance information can be gleaned from national and regional arts organisations. The Arts Council of England is at 14 Great Peter Street, London SW1 and its Web site, www.artscouncil.org.uk, provides links to regional organisations. The Arts Council of Northern Ireland is at MacNeice House, 77 Marlow Road, Belfast BT9 6AQ, www.artscouncil-ni.org, and the Arts Council for Wales at 9 Museum Place, Cardiff CF10 3NX, www.ccc-acw.org.uk.

Keep up with cutting edge practitioners by visiting your local receiving theatre or checking out places like the Institute for Contemporary Art (ICA), The Mall, London SW1Y 5AH, www.ica.org.uk, or The Green Room, Whitworth Street, Manchester, www.u-net.com/set/greenroom.

Fairground operator

Travelling funfair rides are generally a family business, run by people who are born and brought up in the nomadic life. However, it is possible to buy new or used touring fairground rides and vehicles and take to the road yourself. For some it can be viewed as a gruelling life – living out of caravans, setting up and taking down rides in all weathers and making just enough money to get by. However, the travel and excitement of the fairground can be unbeatable.

For those who enjoy the fun of the fair and love people to scream if they want to go faster, but would rather avoid the nomadic life, there is an alternative. The rise of the theme park has made it possible to find full- and part-time jobs in running amusement rides.

Many theme parks are owned by national companies who have resorts and attractions nationally and internationally. Each year these parks are in competition with one another, trying to attract more customers through more incredible rides and offering more exciting experiences. These experiences may include elements such as themed hotels – as seen at Alton Towers – or all-in-one travel packages such as those offered by Disney. Alongside the rides at a place like a Disney theme park, entertainers and character performers are employed to entertain visitors as they move from ride to ride.

In whatever context they work, ride operators are employed to make sure the riders are safely fastened in their seats before the ride begins. They must ensure the attraction is safe before each ride and know what to do if there are any problems. They may also need to advise customers not to take the ride should height or health restrictions apply.

There may be smaller, more locally based resorts where you can work alongside fairground attractions. The scale of operation here means you are likely to have more responsibility for the site than you would if a large company employed you and so understandably you will need a wider variety of skills to do the job.

The rides themselves are designed and constructed by specialist construction firms. Artists and designers working here require specialist engineering skills to ensure the ride works safely and consistently. Designers can also find work in creating the theme park environment in which these rides will be positioned. If a ride is designed properly it should be possible for onlookers to feel involved with it before they get on board.

 Highs: Giving customers a unique and exciting experience.

 Lows: When it rains your customers are unlikely to turn up, but you still have to set up the ride and take it down again. Sometimes travelling fairground operators are charged for damage done to the site if heavy vehicles have churned up the ground.

Facts, links and trivia

The National Fairground Archive is held at Sheffield University and can be explored online at www.shef.ac.uk/nfa. While *The World's Fair* magazine, with an editorial office at 2 Daltry Street, Oldham, Lancashire OL1 4BB (tel: 0161 6243687) carries news and adverts for new and used rides, *The Fairground Mercury* – with its editorial office at 5 Crooks Lane, Studley, Warwickshire B80 7QX – is the official publication of the Fairground Association of Great Britain. The Association also runs a comprehensive Web site of useful links and current news at www.fagb.co.uk. Alton Towers is run by the Tussaud's Group and its Web site is at www.alton-towers.co.uk.

In recent years, old-style steam driven touring fairs have gained in popularity. Families seem to enjoy the novelty and history of these kinds of rides more than the hassle and speed of modern rides. However, such attractions bring with them extra costs in terms of maintenance and when your only source of income is through the number of people who get on your ride, you may want a simpler attraction.

Stand-up comedian

A few years ago comedy was billed as 'the new rock and roll'. Anyone could get on stage and do his or her 10 minutes and if the act was good, fame and fortune were waiting. All you needed was enough guts to get up there and do it in the first place. Today the opportunity for getting up and showing off still exists, but the comedy scene is now awash with 'wannabe' comedians so becoming a top stand-up comic requires limitless enthusiasm, bags of commitment and not a little talent.

London has a thriving comedy circuit of small pub rooms and a few dedicated clubs where new comedians can get up and try to make people laugh. Some of these places have a proper PA system and microphone; others have nothing more than a single amplifier and speaker while still others will not even bother with lights or microphones at all. The aspiring comedian starts by phoning up the bookers at these clubs and travels round each venue many times, doing as many gigs as possible and trying to impress the audience and the bookers. At first, these spots will only last for five minutes maximum but even this can seem like an eternity to the comic who has bad material.

The comic must show bookers that they are keen to improve their act, that they are trying out new material and that they want to succeed in the business. Gradually, they may be offered other 'open mic' slots on more high profile dates. They may eventually start getting paid gigs from bookers who like their act. In order to create a national profile they need to be ready to travel around the country, often still doing only five minutes, resulting in extremely late nights and a substantial travel budget. Many stand-ups go to the Edinburgh Festival each year, financing their own shows to promote their talent. Edinburgh can be seen as a trade fair for bookers and there may be many people there on the lookout for new talent to develop TV or radio shows.

To be successful in the world of stand-up you need a certain amount of chance and luck as well as talent and skill. You need to be in the right place at the right time and talking to the right people. It can appear that comedians – like pop stars – are overnight successes, but frequently such overnight success has been preceded by many years of toil doing hard gigs, dying on stage and wondering whether what you are doing is actually funny at all.

 Highs: Having a good night on stage where everyone loves you.

 Lows: Having to phone round venues again in order to book more gigs.

Facts, links and trivia

Successful stand-ups can travel the world – there is a thriving circuit for playing to ex-pat workers in places like Hong Kong and even Saudi Arabia. Such performances are all expenses paid – flights, accommodation and subsistence expenditure while you are there – as well as netting hundreds of pounds for two or three gigs.

Check your local listings magazines for comedy venues and start phoning around to see if they take 'open mic' performers. *Time Out* in London, *Venue* in Bristol and *City Life* in Manchester all carry comedy listings. On the Web you can search for your favourite comedian or stop off at any of a number of comedy portals. www.chortle.co.uk is particularly useful for news and reviews as well as offering advice for new starters. www.comedyonline.co.uk also provides comprehensive information about clubs and performers across the UK.

Role-player/mystery shopper

Used for the training and assessment of staff, role-players and mystery shoppers have one of the more devious jobs in the world of business and retail. Training staff to deal with customers or indeed, training staff to deal with other members of staff, is important to companies who want to put the customer first and maximise the efficiency of their organisation. Role-players are employed either covertly or explicitly to help employers assess the way their employees handle customers and fellow members of staff. If used explicitly the employee realises the interview is a test and will try to behave appropriately, showing off his or her people skills to the full. Such an interview could be used as part of a recruitment test or may simply be there to assess the employee's skills and suggest areas for improvement. In some cases the interview may be stopped and restarted for the employee to try different approaches to the same problem.

Alternatively, the employee may have no idea that the person he or she is dealing with is not a 'real' member of the public. A mystery shopper may be used to carry out a specific transaction with a member of staff and to report back on how effectively the employee dealt with the situation. Mystery shoppers could be used by the employing organisation or may be sent by a third party in order to survey the quality of services on offer from a variety of suppliers. A magazine could review the customer service standards of a number of chemists, for example, measuring them for knowledge and helpfulness.

Role-playing is particularly common in the financial world where there are many rules and regulations that must be observed by suppliers when dealing with customers. There are definite pieces of information which have to be stated to and understood by the customer when, for example, dealing with mortgages. Often, the outcome of a role-play interview will affect the future career of an individual so it is important that the role-player should be impartial and fair when conducting an interview – not just creating problems for the sake of it.

There are a few role-playing agencies in the UK who look to take on actors as role-players. However, you may also be able to find work by approaching companies directly. The training department of retail banks, for example, may indicate whether they use role-players for developing their staff.

 Highs: Using acting skills in a lucrative and constructive way to give participants real skills.

 Lows: Acting out the same role many times can become boring.

Facts, links and trivia

Wheelie Serious, a chain of bike shops (www.wheelie-serious.com) actually offer cycle shoppers a £50 voucher to spend on their merchandise if they fill out a feedback form after shopping at one of Wheelie Serious' high street branches. Meanwhile, a more professional mystery shopping and service analysis company can be found at www.Aba.co.uk. This is the Web site for Aba Quality Monitoring Ltd, 2 Parkfield Road South, Didsbury, Manchester M20 6DA. The company designs and executes tailor-made quality monitoring programmes for a wide range of clients. Assessment can be carried out either in person or over the phone.

Actors in Management, www.actoirsinmanagement.com, provides role-playing services with a difference to corporate customers. The difference is that all the company's role-players have had direct experience in business management themselves so are coming at the discipline from an informed point of view rather than simply being there to be difficult. The organisation can be reached via the Web site or at 43 Coleraine Road, London N8 0QJ.

Professional look-alike

You will need an amount of good luck in the looks department to be successful at this job. At the same time simply looking like someone famous is not guaranteed to earn you a living. You will need to be able to enter into the spirit of the person you look like – creating an entire performance that makes your act believable and helps people enjoy what you do. You will need to act and perform. You may need to sing or even make public speeches.

Look-alikes are used on a wide range of occasions. They may be used for corporate events, advertising campaigns, modelling work or for public engagements. They might appear to liven up private parties and increasingly there is a trend for look-alike and sound-alike tribute bands playing the music of many popular groups.

A quick scan of the back page of *The Stage* newspaper reveals the number of look-alikes available – royalty, TV personalities, film stars (both alive and dead) – as well as tribute bands to The Beatles, ABBA and many others. Alarmingly, sound-alike bands are sprouting up playing the songs of contemporary artists – there is already a Steps tribute band to join the U2 tribute bands and others. *The Stage* is also a good source to find the contact details of agencies and management companies who deal with look-alikes.

Being a look-alike can mean international work and film work. You may find yourself working long hours just as any other performer and you may find the constant act of being someone else very tiring. Some look-alikes find it frustrating that they cannot actually get any work as themselves – they must always appear as their look-alike. Success here is absolutely linked to the popularity of the character they are playing. If the character falls out of favour or is forgotten then the look-alike is likely to be out of work. Moreover, it can be difficult – although not impossible – to switch to being a different, more popular look-alike. When their star finally falls, some look-alikes remain in the entertainment business, becoming agents and artist managers themselves.

 Highs: Being treated as a famous person.

 Lows: Not being wanted to perform as you; typecasting.

Facts, links and trivia

If you can't find a copy of *The Stage* in your newsagents, the editorial office is at 47 Bermondsey Street, London SE1 3XT (tel: 020 7403 1818) and the Web site is at www.thestage.co.uk. Anyone who starts working in performance – whether on stage or for personal appearances – should become a member of the actor's union Equity: Guild House, Upper St Martin's Lane, London WC2H 9EG (tel: 020 7379 6000) www.equity.org.uk; and musicians should join the Musicians' Union, 60 Clapham Road, London SW9 0JJ (tel: 020 7852 5566) www.musiciansunion.org.uk.

While you brush up on your impersonations, check out the competition by visiting a couple of agency Web sites such as www.simply-the-best-entertainment.co.uk/lookalike.html (its offerings include 'The Trotter Family Mk II' from *Only Fools and Horses*) or www.abbauk.co.uk – a tribute site to a tribute band.

**Here's
Health**

Interest in complementary medicine has been increasing over many years as individuals search out new approaches and treatments that fit their lifestyle. While the British Medical Association (BMA) may not recognise some of these treatments, they are gaining popularity among general practitioners, some of whom have even trained in these subjects and are able to offer them alongside the usual service. In the next year or so some of these practices will be recognised by the Department of Health with the result that there will be specific training requirements to be met by professional practitioners. Meanwhile complementary medicine disciplines continue to be policed by their own regulatory bodies, which recognise both the training centres that specialise in that area of medicine and the individuals qualified to practise. These organisations should be your first port of call for finding out more about the area of treatment in which you are interested and how you can get started.

You should be aware of a few points surrounding this area of work. Firstly, there is usually a great deal of training involved requiring large amounts of your time, energy and finance. Once you have completed your training you may still need to fork out additional finance for registering fees, equipment, materials, and most importantly, insurance. You cannot take the risk of practising on members of the public without being insured against the times when things go wrong.

Secondly, these practices still require a high standard of academic work, especially in the area of human biology. It is impossible to work in any complementary medical practice without understanding how the body works. Thirdly, many – but not all – of the people who do take up a job as a practitioner in alternative medicine do so as a second career. This is partly due to the financial requirement and partly because of the experience and life skills one needs in order to be a successful practitioner in this area. Practitioners need a level of maturity, partly to gain the confidence of their patients – which school-leavers may find hard to demonstrate.

Finally, being a successful practitioner requires another completely different set of skills. Alternative and complementary medical practitioners tend to be self-employed, running individual practices from home if not from dedicated surgeries. The individual must therefore be able to be his or her own boss, managing the financial and promotional side of the activity and ensuring the work does not take over his or her entire life. A number of practitioners set up surgeries with each other in order to spread the task of attracting patients, while splitting overheads and running costs.

In general, complementary health practitioners will receive about £35 per appointment with each appointment lasting between 30 minutes and an hour. More technical or demanding practices may command fees around £50 per hour appointment. If you were able to see seven patients a day at £35 each you could clear £245. However, preserving your own health and sanity makes this impossible. You need to strike a balance between the income you receive and the amount of work you do. You may be inspired by the idea of homeopathy, but if you do nothing but talk and prescribe all day you will soon be tired of the work or find the standard of your care is dropping. Given this, it is wise to do a quick bit of mathematics before embarking on your chosen profession.

Chiropodist

Many people pay no attention to their feet. They just assume the bits on the end of their legs will take care of themselves. However, healthy feet are often the key to an individual's all-round happiness. If walking or standing is uncomfortable then the whole posture of an individual can be affected. Chiropodists have been around for many years taking care of all medical problems associated with the feet. They will remove bunions, treat calluses and verrucas or simply give the foot a clean up and massage. Their work can prevent in-growing toenails and help people walk properly and in comfort.

Chiropodists can work from dedicated private clinics or may operate a mobile service, travelling to patients with their own equipment and carrying out their work in the patient's home. Unsurprisingly, patients tend to be old people – pensioners who are no longer able to look after their feet and who may suffer from problems due to walking badly. However, chiropody has gained some popularity with younger people, keen to get the benefits of well looked-after feet. Chiropodists may also work in the sports world and even the theatre – professional ballet dancers, for example, rely on their feet for their livelihood and need help and support to look after them.

A full medical qualification is not necessary for the work, but it is necessary to have scientific knowledge at the GCSE level before you will be accepted on a training course. Many colleges run chiropody programmes – both residential and distance learning – and the Scholl organisation also runs training programmes based around their network of high street shops. Training is split between the classroom and on-the-job practice – watching how it is done and then practising under the watchful eye of a professional.

Chiropodists must be very good communicators, able to reassure and talk to their patients while carrying out the work.

Chiropodists should also be aware that the condition of the feet could be symptomatic of a greater problem – from the wrong type of footwear to more serious medical conditions.

 Highs: Watching someone who has hobbled into the chiropodist's chair walk comfortably away.

Lows: Extracting eight bunions in one go.

Facts, links and trivia

There is no difference between a chiropodist and a podiatrist. Some chiropodists may argue otherwise (usually claiming podiatrists carry out more invasive work) but when it comes down to it, they can all do the same procedures.

There are several professional bodies that govern the practice of Chiropody. These include: The British Chiropody and Podiatry Association, The Association of State Registered Chiropodists, The Institute of Chiropodists and Podiatrists and the Association of Chiropodists and Podiatrists. The majority of professionals are registered with The Society of Chiropodists and Podiatrists stationed at: 1 Fellmonger's Path, Tower Bridge Road, London SE1 3LY (tel: 020 7234 8620) with a Web site at: www.feetforlife.org. Scholl's Web site is at http://193.129.71.65/schollDocs/index.html.

In spite of the existence of all these organisations providing recognition and registration services for professional chiropodists, it is still not actually illegal to claim to be a chiropodist even if you are untrained. This will change over the next 12–18 months, however, as the Department for Health reconsiders the status of complementary medicine.

Trichologist

Trichology is the diagnosis and treatment of diseases and disorders of the hair and scalp. The word derives from the Greek *trichos* meaning hair. Trichology does not just mean trying to come up with the best cure for baldness. In the trichologist's work, the health of the skin on the scalp is as important as the hair. For this reason they may need to treat flaky or oily skin conditions as well as hair loss. Few people realise the importance of their hair – until it starts to fall out. We may think of it as purely a cosmetic feature, but it can be crucial if an individual is to be happy with his or her personal appearance. Like it or not, we place a great deal of importance on the style of our hair and so problems in this area can cause acute embarrassment, leading to low self-esteem and even serious depression.

At the same time, the condition of the hair and scalp can indicate more serious medical conditions. The trichologist may need to carry out thyroid tests to rule out problems and to gain a better idea of what may be causing the trouble. Dealing with such cases clearly requires maximum tact and understanding.

Trichologists work alone, or may set up clinics with other trichologists, but as they are self-employed they are responsible for advertising and attracting their own customers. Since hair plays such an important part in personal identity and presentation it is clear that practising trichologists must be extremely good with people in discussing problems and selecting the right treatment for them. Job satisfaction comes from treating the condition and seeing the improvement in the whole person, not just the hair.

Every patient for the trichologist is different. Similar people may present with hair loss, but techniques such as transplantation do not suit everybody. It is imperative that the trichologist establishes a detailed case history for every patient in order to prescribe the best course of treatment. There may be stress or environment-related issues causing the problem. Sometimes hair can change colour due to minerals or chemicals added to swimming pool water. Any ointments, lotions or special shampoos required by patients are created by the trichologist themselves.

Another growing area of trichologists' work is in the legal field. Too often hair treatments carried out in hairdressers or at home leads to dissatisfaction and even long-term damage. At the same time, hairdressing clients may try taking their hairdressers to court when really the damage that has occurred is not linked to the hairdressers at all. While time-consuming and tiring, in our increasingly litigious society the demands for trichologists to appear as expert witnesses are increasing.

 Highs: Helping to treat hair conditions and improving the appearance of people.

 Lows: Some conditions are not treatable.

Facts, links and trivia

The Institute of Trichologists, www.trichologist.org.uk, 228 Stockwell Road, London SW9 9SU (tel: 08706 070602) recognises qualified individuals in this area and even runs its own three-year training course for new entrants. The course requires two A levels and at least a GCSE in one science-based subject. However, the Institute also runs a foundation course that takes students without those qualifications to the standard required for the full course. The course itself covers biology, microscopy, organic and inorganic chemistry as well as special modules on the structure and make-up of the hair. It is distance learning for the first year with direct experience at a trichology clinic over the following two years.

The profession attracts some young people and a few from hairdressing – it seems concern for the cosmetic side of the hair can lead to wanting to be able to treat the health of the hair too. The London Institute of Trichology, PO Box 142, Stevenage, Herts SG1 5UX, can provide information about anything to do with hair, including latest medical treatments.

Herbalist

The knowledge and use of herbal remedies goes back way over a century. As with many complementary medicines, herbalism takes a holistic approach to health and disease, addressing the entire body rather than simply identifying and treating symptoms alone. To this end, the herbalist begins treatment with a full consultation for each patient, gathering information about all aspects of his or her life. This information includes the individual's diet, habits and lifestyle as well as details of the specific complaint that led the patient to consult the herbalist in the first place.

Herbalism seeks to restore health in human beings through the use of medicinal plants. It is clearly a more 'natural' way of treating conditions than conventional courses of drugs. Indeed, herbalism avoids the problems that can arise through adverse reactions to conventional treatment. At the same time, it is wise to avoid certain herbs and remedies at particular times. Pregnant women in particular should avoid certain compounds as they can adversely affect their child.

Training to become a herbalist is extensive and there are a number of colleges and universities that offer courses in this area. In some cases a four-year full-time course towards a BSc in Phytotherapy requires pre-entrance qualifications of good GCSE passes including English and A level passes in at least two subjects. The College of Phytotherapy has also designed a part-time course but this takes five years to complete. Each course includes in-depth study of medicinal plants and their effects on the human body as well as their preparation and prescription. During the course, trainee herbalists also receive coaching in consulting techniques and diagnosis to ensure they get the right information from patients to prescribe suitable treatment.

With such a long and expensive training period, anyone who wants to enter this area of work must be passionate about herbalism, regarding it as a vocation rather than just a job. Once qualified, herbalists may work as peripatetic doctors – travelling between patients and treating them on site – or they may establish their own surgery.

 Highs: Treating illness with nature.

 Lows: Herbalism is one of the less well-known areas of complementary medicine and you may experience a low number of patients.

Facts, links and trivia

The reason why herbalism is considered an effective medical methodology is because by taking an extract of a substance, the patient's body absorbs that substance more rapidly than through conventional medicines, where the active ingredient may be only a small percentage of the medicine consumed.

Herbalism reflects the origins of pharmacy and can be traced back to the Roman Empire of around 100 AD and the appearance of a book called *De Materia Medica* written by a military doctor which describes more than 600 remedies based on extracts from the natural world. The basic principles of herbalism have remained intact in spite of advances in the knowledge of human biology and medical science. Today, many herbal remedies are created through the combination of traditional teaching with contemporary research in medicine and pharmaceuticals. First contact for courses should be The College of Phytotherapy, Bucksteep Manor, Bodle Street Green, Near Hailsham, East Sussex BN27 4RJ (tel: 01323 834800).

Acupuncturist

While the practice of acupuncture still goes unregulated in the UK, it is good to know that regulatory bodies do exist. Between them, the British Acupuncture Council (BAcC) and the British Acupuncture Accreditation Board define and recognise standards for both education in and the practice of acupuncture. Formed in 1995, the BAcC brought together five groups and created a common code of practice, shared ethics and discipline procedures for its members. This unification of representative bodies is just as well since acupuncture is one of the more invasive complementary treatments one can receive, involving the insertion of needles into the skin at strategic areas of the body. Given this, the need for professional recognition and representation for the public is paramount.

Acupuncture is based on traditional Chinese philosophy that health comes from the smooth and balanced flow of the body's motivating energy known as Qi. Qi flows through a series of meridians or channels beneath the skin and is made up of equal and opposite qualities – Yin and Yang. When Yin and Yang are unbalanced there may be illness within the patient. By inserting needles into the patient's body, the acupuncturist can stimulate the body's own healing responses and thus restore the natural balance. The flow of Qi could be disrupted by a number of different factors including emotional states such as anxiety, stress and grief or through more physical factors: poor nutrition, infections and trauma. Thus acupuncture can treat all manner of conditions within patients – helping to relieve pain, depression and even helping people overcome addictions to smoking, alcohol and food.

As in other areas of complementary medicine, acupuncture takes a holistic approach, treating the entire body rather than specific symptoms. The acupuncturist will therefore establish a clear case history before commencing treatment that could range from studying the shape and appearance of the tongue through to dietary and medical issues.

Many patients have preconceptions about what acupuncture involves and they may be nervous about what will happen. The acupuncturist will need to provide reassurance before commencing treatment. There are around 500 acupuncture points on the body, 100 of which are most commonly used and while needles are usually associated with the treatment, acupuncture can be used for babies and children simply through applying pressure to the relevant points.

Λ Highs: Treating people in a different and interesting way.

V Lows: Overcoming prejudice against this kind of treatment.

Facts, links and trivia

There are many training centres that run a variety of courses in acupuncture up and down the country and The British Acupuncture Accreditation Board (BAAB), 63 Jeddo Road, London W12 9HQ (tel: 0208 735 0466, e-mail: baab@dial.pipex.com) holds a list of recognised training centres. Colleges must complete a 3–5 year Accreditation process before they can train individuals to a standard recognised by the BAAB. The Board also publishes an annual Register of Practitioner Members which lists qualified acupuncture practitioners by geographic area.

The Chinese practice of healing through acupuncture dates back at least 2,000 years, although some claim the figure is more like 4,000 years. Current practice is supported and furthered through the work of the Acupuncture Resource Research Centre (ARRC), 122A Acomb Road, York YO2 4EY which holds around 25,000 records relating to the practice as well as links with the British Library's online system.

Hypnotherapist

Hypnosis is a trance state in which something unusual happens. Essentially, hypnotherapists make suggestions to an individual's mind in order to bring about a change in that person's behaviour. You have probably seen hypnotists on stage or TV putting members of their audience into a trance and then suggesting they are other people or that they carry out certain activities. In hypnotherapy, the patient is placed into a similar suggestive state, but this is then used to address emotional, mental or even physical problems.

Some people feel hypnosis has something mysterious to it, but hypnotherapy is really about using the body's natural mechanisms for change and focusing them in order to benefit the individual. It is not possible to hypnotise someone against their will and once placed in that state the hypnotherapist must only address the issues required by the patient. In the case of smokers who wish to give up smoking, hynotherapists may place a suggestion in the patient's head that cigarettes taste particularly bad. They may give the smoker another suggestion so that he or she automatically refuses cigarettes when they are offered. In both cases, the hypnotherapist is merely offering a technique to help support the patient's own will to give up smoking.

In the case of emotional problems, hypnotherapy can enable the patient to remember significant events from their past which could still be affecting their behaviour today. Under hypnosis this event can be replayed and suggestions made to counter the emotional response from that event.

Applying hypnosis is a skill that people can learn – indeed many doctors and dentists use hypnotherapy for the treatment of pain or anxiety during other treatments. Dealing with emotions and feelings at this level does require very particular people skills. Hypnotherapists must be good communicators and be extremely patient with their clients. They must always be in control of the sessions they run and exude confidence to their patients.

The Hypnotherapy Society claims to be the fastest growing professional organisation for practising hypnotherapists in the UK. Working from the recognition that the profession was suffering from fragmentation – until the creation of the Society, practitioners were simply represented by whichever organisation first trained them – the Society has built up a number of important resources for practitioners including a member's journal, a public liability and professional indemnity insurance scheme and promotional techniques to put members in touch with clients.

 Highs: Enabling people to overcome problems.

 Lows: You may suffer from the suspicion some people attach to hypnosis.

Facts, links and trivia

The Hypnotherapy Society runs an extensive Web site at www.hypnotherapysociety.com. Alternatively the Society can be contacted at P.O. Box 15, Tenterden, Kent TN30 7ZE (tel: 01580 765856). The Society provides accreditation for training schools and so can point you in the direction of a quality local provider. Training to be a hypnotherapist involves learning the process of self-hypnosis so it is important to make sure you are working with a group of people you trust.

According to one source there are five principal causes for phobia: severe stress, the building of a series of negative experiences, fear of fear, transmission from another person and past trauma. Clients who wish to address a personal phobia can be placed under hypnosis in order to track down the origins of their fear. A suggestion can then be made for countering the anxiety they experience.

The stress monitor Web site at http://stress-uk.net carries information and links to articles covering all areas of stress in modern life and how to tackle it. There are links to further information about complementary medicine including hypnotherapy.

Osteopath

Osteopathy is a method of treatment based on the manipulation of the bones. The principles of osteopathy were founded by an American, Andrew Taylor Still, born in Virginia in 1828. In the last part of that century, Still distanced himself from contemporary medicine practice, and developed the view that many diseases and conditions of the body could be aided through the manipulation of the bones and muscles. He developed a methodology based on the idea that manipulating the body directly affects blood flow around the body and therefore the overall medical condition of the individual.

Commonly osteopathy is sought out simply for the treatment of back problems. While this kind of manipulation is certainly an effective way of treating back conditions, it is by no means limited to such ailments. Research continues today to assess the overall direct benefits produced by osteopathic treatments.

Treatment from an osteopath begins with a thorough analysis of the patient's condition. This comprises a physical examination as well as assessing the patient's dietary and living habits. The patient may be asked to perform a set of actions which will help the osteopath to identify strengths and weaknesses in the body. Very often this kind of body language will tell the osteopath more about the patient's condition than the individual is able to report him- or herself.

Training to be an osteopath is a rigorous process, covering consultation and diagnosis backed up with a full knowledge of biology. Anatomy is studied in great detail as well as general pathology (ie the way the body works) and nutrition. Treatment itself is referred to as the neuro-muscular technique and, clearly, students must have a sound grasp of how the body works before they start the hands-on work of manipulation. For this reason, potential osteopaths can look forward to at least three years of training before setting up in practice. They should ideally have three A level passes including Chemistry and Biology, although some colleges will allow entrants who can demonstrate similar levels of competency or experience without official qualifications.

Since treatment is a physical activity osteopaths must be very confident in themselves and with other people's bodies. Osteopaths cannot feel nervous about treating patients and must be able to put them at their ease before, during and after treatment.

 Highs: Helping patients with a real hands-on treatment.

 Lows: Setting up your own practice and getting your own patients can be difficult and time consuming.

Facts, links and trivia

The first UK school of osteopathy was established in 1917 in London, 15 years after Andrew Still inaugurated his own school in Kirksville, Missouri. Today there are around 3,000 practising osteopaths in the UK.

The General Osteopathic Council at Osteopathy House, 176 Tower Bridge Road, London SE1 3LU (tel: 020 7357 6655) is the professional body for the practice and all osteopaths must be registered with the society before they can practise. The organisation runs a useful network of resources at www.osteopathy.org.uk; and interestingly, HRH The Prince of Wales is the council's Patron. The Osteopathic Educational Foundation (OEF) provides interest-free student loans to students who have completed their first year at an osteopathic institution. Application is through referral by the principal of your institution and, consequently, an interview with the OEF.

Homeopath

While the principles and practice of homeopathy date back some 200 years, it is only in the last 20 years or so that formal structures have been introduced to this area of complementary medicine. Essentially, homeopathy entails treating disease by using small amounts of a medicine that, in healthy persons, would produce symptoms similar to that of the disease being treated. This is in accordance with the Law of Similars which lies behind the practice – or to put it another way: 'That which makes sick shall heal.'

The popularity of this form of medicine – amongst patients and practitioners – has increased immensely over recent years and apparently the Royal Family have used homeopathy for generations. Today, homeopathic practice has been greatly improved through the use of IT. Database technology makes cross-referencing substances with the effects they have much easier, and enables comparisons to be made over a huge number of cases. At the same time, electronic communication has brought together what was a diverse and widespread community of practitioners, allowing them to share and develop practice.

Like other complementary medical practitioners, the homeopath begins treatment by gathering information from the patient from all aspects of their life. While patients may attend with specific problems, the homeopath must take other symptoms and the patient's general condition into account. It is part of the homeopath's skill and art as to how this evidence is used.

On the one hand the homeopath may be able to connect physical conditions with emotional and mental symptoms, identifying features of the individual's condition that indicate the body is already trying to heal itself. On the other hand, trying to address too many symptoms may dilute the effect of any medicine administered, with the result that little progress is made in any one area. Having considered the patient's evidence, the homeopath must select the medicine he or she considers will have the best result for that condition. Follow-up sessions may be set on a monthly basis for the homeopath to track the effect of the treatment with the patient and make further recommendations and prescriptions if required.

On a daily basis, the homeopath may hear the problems and conditions of lots of different patients. The homeopath must develop a way of empathising with people – understanding their problems – while not getting too involved and being able to preserve his or her own personal space. They must maintain a professional distance and ensure that they are still paid and still attracting new patients to replace those who are satisfied with their treatment and ready for discharge.

 Highs: Treating patients' conditions and enhancing their health.

 Lows: It takes at least two years to establish a good home-opathic practice and around 80 per cent of trainees do not manage to create such ventures.

Facts, links and trivia

Modern homeopathy was first formulated by a German physician, chemist and linguist called Samuel Hahnemann, but according to the Society of Homeopath's Web site, www.homeopathy-soh.org, its philosophy can be traced as far back as the 16th century to Paracelsius, a philosopher and physician who said: 'Those who merely study and treat the effects of disease are like those who imagine that they can drive away the winter by brushing the snow from the door. It is not the snow that causes winter, but the winter that causes the snow.'

There are over a dozen colleges around the country where homeopathy can be studied. The Society of Homeopaths at 2 Artizan Road, Northampton NN1 4HU (tel: 01604 621400) is one of a few organisations that give professional recognition to homeopaths and it is involved with developing standards for education that will help prospective students to be certain of the standard of training they receive.

Fresh cosmetics maker

The cosmetics world has recently become a battlefield, with companies trying to outdo one another with the freshness and novelty value of cleansing products for the body, face, hair and hands. Out of this have come such wonderful products as the bath ballistic, the solid bubble bath bar, frozen shower gel and moisturising lotion made from hemp. The bath ballistic, if you don't know, is a ball of bicarbonate combined with numerous smelly, relaxing and skin nourishing ingredients which when dropped into a running bath, fizzes and disintegrates, spreading oils, perfumes and nutrients throughout the water. Frozen shower gel is just that – the idea being that the gel melts in an invigorating and refreshing way while you bathe.

Coming up with fresh ideas for the domestic market and creating these products in large numbers requires imagination, some knowledge of chemistry and, at the end of the process, an efficient production line of enthusiastic workers.

Each cosmetic product is designed and created by qualified chemists and trichologists. Not only do they know the health-giving properties of the herbal and chemical substances they use, they will also know how to combine these ingredients in the most exciting way. Today's consumer places great importance on natural ingredients, freshness and novelty.

Once a new product has been shown to be practical it can go into production. Workers making ballistics will mix together the right amount of ingredients, put them into a mould and wait for them to set. Workers must be able to use their own initiative, ensuring the ballistics they make reach the usual standard for the product and changing the ingredients if they do not measure up. At the same time, it is unlikely that you will end up simply making ballistics all day. Cosmetics manufacturers produce a wide range of products so you will need to be a flexible worker, able to work on all the different lines and in different parts of the production process.

While cosmetic product designers may be trained in chemistry or similar disciplines there are opportunities for training and development in this area for production line workers who show an interest. And the designers are always on the lookout for new ideas – no matter where or who they come from. You should start by contacting the manufacturers direct – there may be vacancies within production or in the distribution and marketing side of the company. In many cases, companies are looking for original, off-the-wall approaches to marketing which will get the public revelling in their luxury bath products. Working on the production line will not immediately enable you to design your own bath products, but you will have the chance to rise through the ranks.

 Highs: Groovy product – and very nice-smelling work place.

 Lows: While you may be moved around the production process, you may still find the work repetitive.

Facts, links and trivia

While Lush cosmetics – www.lush.co.uk, 29 High Street, Poole BH15 1AB – is the leading proponent of bath ballistics, the company hasn't been able to copyright the idea with the result that many other companies – from Boots to small special interest shops – have created their own versions of the product.

Lush has certainly carved out its own niche in the market, but it should be remembered that The Body Shop – www.bodyshop.com – really started the trend in fresh, natural and innovative cosmetics. It is now possible to go on a tour around The Body Shop centre in Littlehampton to see how the company operates. For more information, write to: Body Shop International, Watermead, Littlehampton, West Sussex BN17 6LS (tel: 0800 0960809).

Pest controller

It has been suggested that if a large bomb were dropped on the major cities of the world the only survivors would be the cockroaches. These insects can – and do – get everywhere and once an infestation begins they are extremely difficult to eradicate. However, they can spread dirt and germs and so represent a serious health risk if left to their own devices.

Pest controllers work in both commercial buildings such as shops and offices and private accommodation. They may be employed by the local council's hygiene department or work for a commercial company delivering services to a wide variety of clients. Controllers do not need to know about the hazards they will deal with before entering the profession. Thorough training is given so they can identify the particular type of pest causing the problem – and there are many different types of cockroaches, mites, bugs and insects which can cause problems – before deciding on the best course of treatment for the infestation. Treatment can mean using chemical sprays or powders or even fumigating an area, but it is equally about educating the property owner so that their behaviour does not encourage a reinfestation.

Pest controllers therefore use technical skills for identifying and treating the problem and interpersonal skills for reassuring clients, telling them what the problem is and how they can help. Going into someone's home in order to deal with an infestation requires a huge amount of diplomacy, especially as the home owner might feel they are being personally blamed for the problem – and in practice, they frequently are personally to blame. Handling problems in the commercial sector is even more demanding. Food stores and restaurants can attract many different kinds of pest – a fact which the retailer will not want his or her customers to know.

Controllers must be able to work well on their own. They may be under the supervision of an area manager who will allocate work and provide support, but essentially it is a one-person operation – you as controller versus the pest. The job is not for the squeamish –

some infestations can be gut churning – and given that infestations are usually the result of unhygienic conditions in the first place the working environment is never going to be pleasant. Within commercial pest control organisations there are also opportunities to leave the fieldwork behind and move into the role of technician where you may be studying the habits of rats, mice and roaches in order to develop more effective treatments for the future.

 Highs: Creating a pest-free and hygienic environment.

 Lows: Trying to persuade property owners to take responsibility and change their practices to prevent reinfestation.

Facts, links and trivia

There are around 3,500 different species of cockroach but the most common by far is the German cockroach. This pest can be found in domestic locations, supermarkets and even hospitals. It can be introduced to an environment through contaminated packaging or food and live in secluded locations – behind and underneath cupboards, appliances etc. The female lays 30–50 eggs at a time, and these eggs hatch in about one month. The nymphs start reproducing after between six weeks and four months. The German cockroach produces more eggs per year than any other roach, making infestations particularly difficult to eradicate.

In spite, or perhaps because of the work it carries out, Rentokil-Initial has attained a very high reputation within industry. Not only is it admired by public and industry alike for getting out there and doing the jobs no one else wants to, but its employment practices successfully attract and retain staff in the profession. The company runs a great Web site at www.rentokil-initial.com and be sure to check out the research and development pages which include a rolling list of facts (wash your hands after going to the toilet and reduce the amount of bacteria on your hands by 80 per cent) as well as 'useful' information about the pests you'll be up against.

Funeral director

Many people who work with death every day do it because they want to work with people. Not dead people, of course, but with those who are left to grieve. It is easy to see why. Death is a profoundly moving experience and can be tragic and heart-breaking. As a funeral director, you are able to help people through this difficult period, help them to say farewell to the person who has died and to begin the rest of their lives. Funeral directors effectively stage-manage the funeral – a ritual which marks the end of one person's life and which is as much a celebration of that life as it is a sorrowful occasion.

Funeral directors deal with the entire process of the funeral, taking care of the deceased's body from the point of death through to burial or cremation. They will collect the body from hospital, the mortuary or from a private address. An embalmer may treat the body so it does not decay and is still presentable to relatives if they wish to pay their last respects. There is a lot of customer-centred work to be done – details of the coffin, the service and even the tombstone or memorial must be decided. Eliciting and acting upon this information needs expert people skills to ensure customers explain exactly what they want even though they may be upset and grieving.

On the day itself, it is up to the funeral director to see that all runs smoothly. He or she needs to ensure the vehicles are ready – the hearse and cars for transporting the relatives – that all floral tributes are collected and transported where necessary and that the mourners arrive at the crematorium or church at the right time.

Funeral directors usually receive training on the job, gaining skills and experience with a particular company and gaining more responsibilities as time goes on. The Co-operative Society are well known for their funeral service and run many courses to develop their employees in the job. The society began offering the service over 75 years ago, when it was simply the Portsea Island Mutual Co-operative Society. It introduced the service because it wanted to be able to look after its members 'from cradle to grave'. At the same time, there are many small funeral directing firms that serve local areas and these will provide you with details of how to apply for work.

 Highs: Helping people at a time of great need.

 Lows: Can be depressing – you need to be a particular sort of person to get ongoing job satisfaction from the work.

Facts, links and trivia

The British Institute of Funeral Directors, at 140 Leamington Road, Coventry CV3 6JY, is responsible for the registration, training and examination of tutors within the profession. Since funeral directors do not need any licence to trade it is important to make sure your skills have professional recognition. Director companies should also be members of the Funeral Standards Council (tel: 01222 382046) who run a code of practice for the funeral industry.

The Co-operative Society's funeral directors can be found at: www.funeralcare.co.uk. The National Association of Funeral Directors can be found at www.nafd.org.uk and 618 Warwick Road, Solihull, West Midlands B91 1AA (tel: 0121 7111343). As is usually the way with caring jobs, the profession is substantially undervalued in terms of pay with directors' weekly pay beginning at around £250.

**With
Great
Interest**

Turning your hobby into a job can lead you into strange areas of work. You may discover you are able to work offering services to other people who share your interest. Any magazine or information service that you use on a regular basis will prove useful to you, carrying specific vacancies, advertisements from people already offering services and by indicating areas where a new service would be feasible. Alternatively, as a fanatic yourself, you may be all too aware of areas for business opportunities serving other interested people. If there's an area where you would like to be better served – whether it is receiving more information about certain aspects of your interest or an opportunity to buy related merchandise – why don't you set up the service?

The Internet is a great arena for this kind of venture. By linking people together from all over the world it has been possible to create new communities of people who share similar interests. It doesn't matter if those interests are obscure or unfathomable by the rest of the world; the Internet offers you the chance to contact millions of people, giving you a great marketplace for your business. Making money from this doesn't just mean selling merchandise around the world – indeed, you may not need to sell anything at all. You could start by simply running a news list or a forum where members can share ideas and opinions on your interest – if it is successful there may be established businesses who want to advertise on the site, tapping into a specific group of people who may be more disposed to buying their product than the general public would be. By uniting people with a shared interest, you can provide the perfectly targeted market into which other companies can sell.

You may not be particularly interested in the areas listed below, but use these examples to help you think about your own passion – whether it is for music, railways or model making – and try to think of roles you could take in the supply chain from supplier to customer. There is only one danger with turning your hobby into a job and that lies in the fact that hobbies are usually separate from daily working life. The reason for this has also been that the hobby is something you do for pleasure, away from the daily grind. Put the two together and turn your interest into part of the daily routine, you could lose all enthusiasm for the subject.

Taxidermist

While for some the idea of preserving and displaying a dead animal seems macabre, taxidermy is a way of making nature more accessible to be studied and experienced. A well-presented specimen can be encountered in a way which would be impossible if the animal were still alive.

There are many preconceptions about what a taxidermist does, and many of these date back to the Victorian age when the only way to prove the existence of a certain animal was to kill and preserve a specimen. Taxidermy itself became very fashionable and some specimens were prized more than others, resulting in the price for that specimen rising and a premium being paid for suitable new corpses. In some instances, the market for a stuffed specimen actually contributed to the extinction of the animal itself.

Today, taxidermists operate in a far more honourable and professional manner. The majority of specimens come from accidental deaths – usually road kills – and all buying and selling should only be carried out with suitable paperwork proving where the specimen came from and the name of the taxidermist.

The job of the taxidermist is a very skilled one, requiring artistic talent and knowledge about natural history as well as preservation and mounting techniques. The taxidermist will start the process of mounting a specimen by skinning the dead animal or bird and preserving the skin. This is done using a number of chemicals and techniques. The taxidermist repairs any damage which might have occurred to the skin during the animal's life (or death) and then either creates or selects a mould for that animal on which the skin can be placed. There is no 'stuffing' carried out by taxidermists. The models on which the skins are mounted are usually moulded in plastic so the taxidermist's skill lies in putting mould and skin together.

The taxidermist will ensure the pose of the animal represents the animal's natural behaviour. To do this, the taxidermist must have a good knowledge of anatomy and of the behaviour of the animals he or she is working with.

Becoming a skilled taxidermist requires time and dedication. It is a skill to be learnt first hand from a professional, gaining experience with different techniques as well as a variety of subjects. By joining the Guild of Taxidermists you can get in touch with current practitioners as well as working towards recognised taxidermy qualifications. The qualifications are based on the rewarding of 'standard credits' – given for each piece of professionally created taxidermy. Accreditation then ranges from being an Accredited Member of the Guild to being a specialist in a particular field of taxidermy – bird, mammal, fish, game for example – to becoming a master taxidermist in a particular field. There are only a few master taxidermists in the UK today.

 Highs: Preserving wildlife for future generations to enjoy.

 Lows: Dealing with dead animals can be distressing, and in some cases the animals may be too badly damaged to be preserved.

Facts, links and trivia

While working for a company of taxidermists might earn you a basic wage, it is worth bearing in mind exactly how much money you can get through individual jobs. The preserved hide of a fox, for example, could net £50 while the fully presented body is worth around £250. A stag's head (shoulder mounted) is worth upwards of £400 while the entire animal commands prices upwards of £1200.

The Booth Museum in Brighton, at 194 Dyke Road BN1 5AA (tel: 01273 292777) is worth a visit for any aspiring taxidermist.

It is the creation of Edward Booth, a Victorian ornithologist whose collection of stuffed British birds forms the centre of the collection. Today there's everything from a pygmy shrew to a killer whale so if you come away feeling excited rather than freaked out, taxidermy is probably the profession for you. If this is the case proceed directly to the Guild of Taxidermists: c/o Museum and Art Gallery, Kelvingrove, Glasgow G3 8AG.

Philatelist

Stamps have been collectors' items for many years and while the typical collector may be male and in his fifties or sixties, collectors are by no means limited to this profile of the population. Stamps are collected all over the world and from countries all over the world, with enthusiasts keen to complete collections from particular geographical areas, of certain denominations and even of particular subjects – stamps which carry pictures of planes, trains or automobiles, for example.

Stanley Gibbons is the UK's largest trading company in stamps and runs a shop and showroom in London at 399 The Strand WC2R 0LX (tel: 020 7836 8444). The company serves national and international customers through a mail order service as well as producing monthly and annual publications about stamps. Some employees at Stanley Gibbons get to travel all over the world in search of stamps to add to the company's stock. They may attend auctions for particular ranges of stamps or strike deals with obscure but competent suppliers.

While collecting stamps for fun may entail tracking down your own particular preferences, doing it for profit means building up a good stock and maintaining a strong and up-to-date view of the stamp market. The value of a stamp will not just depend on its rarity, but there are fashions and trends here just as in any other retail trade. Market demand will determine whether it is possible to sell a stamp regardless of its condition or whether collectors will buy only mint issues. If there are only a few examples of a certain stamp and everyone wants one, it is clear that collectors will buy regardless of their condition.

There are many small privately run stamp-trading companies in the UK, some run on a part-time basis. Working for such a trader will give you ongoing access to the market. It may not be particularly inspiring work – you may just be completing mail order services – but you may also have the opportunity to design promotions where enthusiasts sign up to receive stamps which form a particular collection. Success in this kind of working environment requires a combination of the enthusiast's knowledge alongside effective business skills. Traders must be able to negotiate a good deal for their stock and put together attractive packages for customers.

There are opportunities to take this market to the Internet – using this as a retail and information outlet that would be more accessible to customers than a single high street location. Naturally, you should bear in mind the age and profile of your principle market (the target customers may not have access to a computer and may not trust financial interactions across the Net) but as time goes by the use of this kind of technology for collecting and contacting like-minded people is certain to grow.

 Highs: Finding rare stamps and putting together promotions.

 Lows: Ensuring you attract sufficient customers to make the business feasible.

Facts, links and trivia

There are many ways you can sell stamps to interested collectors. You can sell through your own local stamp club, at an auction house, a stamp fair or even by holding your own personally run auction. This latter approach means advertising your stock to potentially interested collectors and then stipulating a time and a method by which those collectors can bid for your stock. This may mean running the auction by phone or even a 'blind auction' whereby bidders can make their offers by post with the highest bid getting the stock. In the United States 'Circuit' or Sales Books are used where books of stamps are circulated around potential buyers enabling them to see the goods before buying them.

Stanley Gibbons Monthly is a publication from the eponymous shop which tracks new issues and recent discoveries within the stamp world. It's an absolute must if you are to gauge exactly how valuable your stock is and how desperate other collectors will be to get hold of samples. Stanley Gibbons also runs its own Web site at www.stanleygibbons.com.

Ornithologist

Enthusiastic ornithologists are sometimes known as 'twitchers' – a term which is considered derogatory by some, but taken with pride by others. Jobs available to birdwatchers range from straightforward administrative posts at nature reserves or with conservation organisations, all the way through to complex research work in the recording and monitoring of birds and their habitats in the wild.

Fieldwork is often carried out on behalf of conservation societies or as part of wider research centred on universities and biological or environmental pressure groups. It could feature basic atlas and mapping work – recording the sightings of particular species – or may rely on the identification of birds by their song alone. Other evidence might be recorded such as nesting sites or the appearance of droppings.

Research is carried out all year round and in all weathers. You can expect to work at any time, day or night, and you may need to work in remote or inhospitable locations. There are many opportunities for voluntary work in this area with local groups of the County Conservation Trusts, the British Trust for Conservation as well as through the British Trust for Ornithology itself.

While practical experience will help you find suitable opportunities, some kind of related qualification is likely to net you more interesting and involving work. A levels in biology or other science subjects will help; so too will further and higher degree level qualifications. Adult education courses may also be useful to back up your interest. Whichever educational institution you attend, you may find the establishment has useful links to research groups or is even involved in carrying out its own research programmes.

Highs: Working alongside birds, studying their habits and the effect of the environment upon them.

 Lows: Working in all weathers, at all times.

Facts, links and trivia

The British Trust for Ornithology, www.bto.org, British Trust for Ornithology, The Nunnery, Thetford, Norfolk IP24 2PU (tel: 01842 750050) runs an ongoing Common Birds Census (CBC) which depends upon volunteer birdwatchers to provide reliable data as to species existing in the UK. This is good experience for any avid twitchers since it requires them to visit a plot of woodland or farmland eight or more times each year and plot sightings of every bird they see on a map. This enables the Ornithology Trust to assess the density of birds across the UK and their habitat preferences.

www.rspb.org.uk is a growing Web site which caters for bird lovers, including details of holidays, birdwatching clubs and even relevant items for sale. In addition the site can provide links to 'ringing groups'. Ringing is the practice of identifying the species and sex of a bird and putting a ring round the bird's leg for identity purposes. Birdwatchers must attend a professional ringing course before engaging in this practice themselves.

Tarot reader

The tarot is a pack of cards used to predict the fortune of or give spiritual insight into individual people. The deck is divided into different suits – much like a conventional pack of cards – and the tarot reader interprets the way in which the enquiring individual draws the cards. This interpretation is intended to give the enquirer an insight into his or her own life in order to make informed decisions about what to do. Guidance may include physical and emotional issues or even career advice.

There are some people who scoff at the idea that a pack of cards can provide any kind of help at all in anyone's life; others, however, feel the tarot does hold special powers and that tarot readers have special gifts. You can learn how to interpret the cards by teaching yourself with a pack from any special interest or mystical shop. You may find a reader who is able to offer tuition, and there are even training resources to be found on the Internet.

Tarot readers may operate from their own home, travel to their clients' homes or even open their own consultation rooms. In the case of the latter, location is extremely important. Tarot readers who set up next to shops selling similarly spiritual or mystical-oriented goods are likely to attract more customers than those next to the supermarket in modern shopping arcades. As well as learning all the cards, understanding their meanings and how their meanings can be interpreted together, if you are going to be a tarot reader you must have exceptional people skills. Enquirers are likely to come to you at moments of crisis or with very important questions they would like answered. They will want to analyse everything you say carefully.

Consultations are usually given on a one-to-one basis and may be tape-recorded by the enquirer to take away and listen to later. As time goes by you will find you are able to sense more about the people who visit you through their body language and appearance – that is not to discredit any mystical gifts you may uncover in yourself as you work with the tarot, just that your intuitive skills will increase as you meet and talk to more clients.

You should be aware that there are some con artists in the field of tarot reading; they may make it difficult for you to gain credibility with some members of the public. Many of the phone line tarot services are nothing more than excuses for companies to make money by keeping callers on premium rate phone lines for long periods of time. In general, however, you will find your customers are already convinced of the positive benefits of tarot reading and will therefore set great store by what you have to say.

 Highs: Helping people make difficult life decisions by using intuition and traditional stories.

 Lows: There may be sceptics who you need to win around.

Facts, links and trivia

It is thought that the tarot originated in northern Italy around 1440 and was used by the nobility. Certainly the symbolism of the cards comes from Medieval and Renaissance Europe. Originally the cards were called *carte da trionfi* (cards of the triumphs) and were hand-painted.

It is possible to sign up for online, telephone or postal correspondence training in tarot reading from The Thoth School of Tarot, 5 Shamrock Street, London SW4 6HF (tel: 020 7385 1169) and you can find out more from the Web site at www.whitecauldron.com. The fairly recently formed Association of Tarot Professionals (ATP) can also be reached via the Web site. This organisation recognises and supports tarot readers at all stages of their careers as well as providing a code of professional conduct.

Zookeeper

Zoos used to have a bad press for incarcerating animals in unsuitable surroundings simply for the fascination of the viewing public. Events such as the Chimpanzee's Tea Party had more to do with entertainment than the well-being of the animals involved. This has changed, however, with zoos and country parks now taking an active role in the preservation of endangered species from around the world and contributing to the conservation effort. Unsurprisingly, many people who work in this area have zoological and biological qualifications – some may even have trained as veterinary surgeons. However, it is quite common to find zookeepers who have picked up the job simply through personal interest and on-the-job training.

Through volunteering and working for nothing at your local zoo or wildlife park, you will gain skills in how to look after and manage the wildlife, gaining the trust of the animals themselves and of the full-time staff – the professional keepers – working on site. You may find you slowly gain more responsibilities in the day-to-day management of certain animals or, alternatively, you may use your experience as grounds to take an academic course in this area. At the same time you can start undertaking vocational training to complement your practical experience. Frequently, new keepers will follow a correspondence course to gain the City and Guilds Certificate in Animal Management. This will provide information on everything you need to look after the animals – from nutrition to the wider role of zoos throughout the world.

Do not expect to be handling the animals from day one – in fact, do not expect to be able to handle the animals at all. These days, keepers prefer to avoid direct contact which could adversely affect the animal, giving it the impression that it is human and causing it to depend less on its natural instincts. At the same time, zoological parks like keepers who will be around for a few years since it means the animals will get to trust those keepers and be happier in their habitat.

Mucking out and food preparation are the most likely tasks you will be given to do. Neither job is particularly glamorous but it is through this kind of routine that problems or changes in animal behaviour can be observed. Keepers now go out of their way to provide as natural a habitat as possible to stimulate each animal and prevent boredom, so you may find yourself able to devise new games for feeding time. Keepers must also deal with the public who visit parks or zoos, answering any questions they may have about an animal and ensuring they do not place themselves or the animals in danger.

 Highs: Watching an animal thrive and procreate, and being able to reintroduce endangered species to their natural habitat.

 Lows: You may have to work for a long time before gaining any great responsibilities.

Facts, links and trivia

The British Veterinary Zoological Society (www.bvzs.org) is part of the British Veterinary Society and is responsible for issues concerning exotic pets and zoo animals. You can contact the organisation at BVZS, 7 Bridgewater Mews, Gresford Heath, Pandy, Wrexham LL12 8EQ. Students can become involved with the society and may find that this contact helps them network to find challenging and satisfying work in this area of animal care. Membership is through recommendation by full members of the society, but brings with it access to cutting edge scientific meetings and a biannual publication including a newsletter and papers from members.

The Zoological Society of London tends to recruit keepers for the summer season only although successful candidates who prove themselves will be considered for permanent positions. Vacancies are usually advertised in the *Evening Standard*, or in specialist magazines such as *Cage and Aviary Birds*, or *Aquarist and Pond Keeper*. The Society can be reached at ZSL, Regent's Park, London NW1 4RY and correspondence should be accompanied with an SAE. The Society's Web page is at www.zsl.org and contains links to jobs and news stories.

Hat maker

Hat makers enter the profession through a variety of interests and with various artistic and craft related qualifications. Some have studied fashion at college and end up specialising in headgear. Others start by studying contemporary design disciplines – there are even courses specifically in 3D design – and again they happen across headwear as one aspect of design work. Interest could even come through a result of working in embroidery or textiles.

Whatever the original inspiration, making hats involves a great deal of skill and patience as well as practice. Sketching out the design of a hat is one thing, but it is quite another to transfer that original idea into an object which will rest safely on someone's head, and does not fall off when they move. It must also look good from every angle. The use of different materials is crucial to the look and feel of a hat. Weight and texture will determine how certain material is used as much as the colour and look of the cloth.

Hat makers can work alone or within established millinery companies. These companies may develop new styles and supply them to high street boutiques. There may be specific lines for specific shops and even orders from those shops for specific headwear which will complement other clothes stock. A new summer collection, for example, is a great opportunity for shops to offer wide brimmed summer hats which use or reflect the material and colours of that range.

The process of making a hat starts with the original idea being sketched out by a designer. Once this is approved, an original pattern will be created from which the hat can be realised. Having made adjustments according to the actual appearance of the headgear, the pattern can then be duplicated for further production. Some workers in larger millinery companies may be dedicated to cutting or assembling parts of the hat. While technically working on a production line, the work cannot be described as boring since these workers are often using traditional and highly skilled techniques to create the hat. Each technique will be linked to the type of material used in the construction of the hat – whether it be straw, silk, gauze or netting.

For some, hats are more of an artistic exhibit than of any practical use and such hat makers usually work alone on a freelance basis, creating very individual designs or taking commissions from customers who want something very special. But while hat makers may principally be drawn to the area of fashion headgear, it should not be forgotten that there is always a strong demand for protective headgear as well. Construction workers, and even sportsmen and women, sometimes require sturdy helmets and the like. While they may not grace any catwalk, they offer an equal challenge in terms of design and the selection of materials. They need to be light but strong, offering suitable protection while still giving the user freedom of movement.

 Highs: Creating a highly visual, individual and portable piece of art.

 Lows: Making a living from the work outside a millinery company may be difficult. Individually commissioned hats command a very high price (reflecting the work you have put in) and unless you build a good reputation, this may not attract a long line of customers.

Facts, links and trivia

Luton football team are known as the Hatters – a reference to the extensive straw hat industry which used to exist in the area. The British Hat Guild is still based there at The Business Centre, Kimpton Road, Luton, Bedfordshire LU2 0LB (tel:

01582 522333) and although its Web site is currently under-going redevelopment (www.hat-guild.org.uk) they can be mailed on info@hat-guild.org.uk.

As mentioned, hat-related design and creation can be studied through a variety of disciplines, but The British School of Millinery run dedicated courses on the craft and are based at 84 Hampden Road, Harrow Weald, Middlesex HA3 5PR (tel: 020 8427 7429). The British Hat Network has created a Web site to improve communications between the industry designer and production company: www.millinery.org. It contains a host of useful links for the industry and claims that hat wearing is on the rise in spite of certain Royal Family members requesting no hats on their wedding invitations.

Bespoke tailor

The made-to-measure, personal suit has become as much a fashion statement and symbol of wealth and status as sports cars and world travel. But while such suits can easily cost upwards of £1,500, they may be considered good value for money. Firstly they are made individually for the customer. Secondly, they use high quality material and if the cut isn't too dated in terms of fashion it will last a lifetime. In support of this long-term relationship with the garment, a good bespoke tailor will not simply make a suit for the customer, but will continue to make adjustments to the suit as the client gets older and physically changes.

Making a suit usually requires three appointments with the client. On the first occasion the client is measured extensively and quizzed on the style, cut and material choice for the garment. Decisions at this stage include issues such as how many buttons should be on the cuffs, whether the fly should be button or zip and the number and position of pockets.

By the second appointment, the tailor, using the measurements taken, will have hand-drawn the pattern for the suit and transferred this pattern to the selected material. The original measurements and pattern will be kept on file for future reference. Having carefully cut out the material and started assembly, the second appointment is where embryonic suit and anxious client are first brought together. By slowly piecing the fabric together on the live model, the tailor can see where adjustments need to be made to the fabric and makes appropriate chalk marks which will be used as a reference guide for the final stages of creation. After this fitting the tailor will take the suit apart again, iron each part of the material and then do the final assembly. Each suit takes up to four full days' work to create.

While it is clearly the tailor's skill which ensures customer satisfaction, it is also important to be able to get on well with customers. The tailor needs to glean a great deal of information about the customer's likes and dislikes with regard to the suit and a constant barrage of questions, including items which the customer may not have considered or think relevant, will not make the experience enjoyable or relaxing. The tailor is there to satisfy the customer and if that means talking about things other than the importance of the waistcoat's cut then so be it.

 Highs: No two garments are the same – you are always working on a unique product.

 Lows: Very competitive marketplace where tailors succeed through personal recommendation and reputation.

Facts, links and trivia

Successful tailors can find themselves in demand all over the world – some Saville Row companies regularly travel to the United States to serve clients there. Bespoke is tailoring not purely for men's suits. Women are increasingly looking at tailor-made items, finding that suits made in this way can be both stylish and practical. A good tailor will be able to create a garment with pockets for carrying cosmetics and mobile phones which will not disrupt the line of the suit.

Training for tailoring can be found in many fashion-oriented colleges. However, don't expect to leave and immediately set up your own tailoring operation. You must be prepared to work hard and learn the trade thoroughly, gaining practical experience before becoming responsible for the make up of an entire suit. In some cases, cutting-tailors specialise in certain disciplines or garments within the suit-making process and gain a reputation for excellence in these fields alone. They may even take work from other tailors who want to offer their clients top quality throughout the suit.

Animal therapist

Just as medical conditions in human beings can be treated in a variety of ways, so can those affecting animals. Difficult behaviour or medical conditions should not always result in another round of pills; indeed, some conditions cannot be treated in this way. Sometimes the problem lies with the pet's owner as much as the pet itself.

The first port of call for any animal in distress is a veterinary consultation. If necessary, the vet can refer the patient on to a trained professional who deals with specific problems. Pet behaviour counsellors work on addressing problematic behaviour in animals. There may be simple problems such as cats spraying in their owners' homes, or horses that refuse to go into trailers for transportation. Alternatively there may be more complex and deep-rooted problems. Animals who have been abused by their previous owners, or who have been abandoned, may find it hard to interact with humans. They may interpret every movement towards them – no matter how gentle or well intended – as a threat.

In each case the counsellor observes the animal's behaviour, arrives at a conclusion as to what the problem is and then makes suggestions as to how the owner can address this behaviour. Usually it requires the owner to change the way he or she relates to the animal and persuading the owner to do this can be difficult. Owners form very close relationships with their pets – even if the pets are misbehaving – and they can take suggestions that interfere with that relationship as criticism of their fitness as owners. It is particularly difficult if owners are currently being over-cautious or spoiling their pets.

Other alternative and complimentary medicine techniques can be used on animals. Physiotherapy, chiropractics and even acupressure (acupuncture without the needles) can be used on animals to improve their physical condition and address aches and pains which appear to be troubling them. Physiotherapy techniques are particularly important if an animal has damaged itself in some way or has mobility problems. Conventional chiropractic treatment works through body manipulation to restore nerve operation and correct the human musculo-skeleton and it has good results with animals too. Indeed, many pet owners and people who work with animals for a living prefer this approach to medicine since it is non-invasive and allows the animal to remain calm during treatment.

 Highs: Helping animals and their owners achieve happiness together.

Lows: It can take time for some therapies to take effect. There may not be a single simple solution to poor behaviour.

Facts, links and trivia

Training for these disciplines does take time. To become an animal physiotherapist, you first need to earn your stripes as a chartered physiotherapist (of the human variety) that means a three or four year degree course resulting in a degree or a diploma. Having done that you'll need to serve two years in general practice before taking postgraduate training in animal therapy. Courses are certified by the Association of Chartered Physiotherapists in Animal Therapy (ACPAT) and students will not be allowed to work unsupervised until they have proven complete competence. Check out the ACPAT Web site on www.acpat.org or write to ACPAT Education, Harestock Stud, Kennel Lane, Littleton, Winchester, Hampshire SO22 6PT.

The Association of Pet Behaviour Counsellors can be reached at PO Box 46, Worcester, WR8 9YS or www.apbc.org.uk. There is currently no recognised route for study, but an academic back-ground in sciences together with extensive experience of working with animals will help. Equinenergy, at www.equinenergy.com or 17 The Abbey, Hammerwood Road, Ashurst Wood, East Grinstead, West Sussex RH19 3SA, offers training to become an Equine Body Worker (physiotherapy for horses).

Protester/campaigns organiser

If there is a cause that you firmly believe in, there may be a way you can combine your belief with making money. Charities and pressure groups rely on the work of volunteers to keep their activities going and to raise awareness of their issues throughout the public arena. While these volunteers may not get paid at first, if you stay with an organisation for long enough and show your commitment you will be in a prime position to take advantage of any opportunities that do arise.

Work at this level is extremely varied. You may be involved in street collections or promotions, enlisting the support of members of the public towards a particular project, or simply raising general awareness. This can be hard work sometimes – some members of the public may not be sympathetic to your viewpoint, might simply not want to know or might not want to donate their hard-earned cash to your cause. On the other hand, the satisfaction of having gained the help or sympathy of even one or two more people can be very rewarding.

If street work does not appeal, some campaigning organisations have very busy back offices that manage and arrange campaigning activities and coordinate the local work with other regional centres around the country. Phone calls and letter writing play an important part in promoting many causes – through press releases, publicity literature, posters or flyers. You may be able to use your imagination to dream up new ways of getting the cause noticed – sponsored events or peaceful demonstrations can grab news coverage.

Full-time and paid positions are usually advertised both internally and externally, but it is clear that having established a track record with the organisation you are likely to be in a good position to apply for full-time work. While unsurprisingly, the charity sector will give lower pay and benefits compared with the commercial sector, it is not an exceptionally low-paying sector. Some pressure groups – the high profile and well-supported organisations – can sometimes match levels of the private sector.

 Highs: Working for something you believe in.

Lows: There is always a danger of 'burnout' in these jobs. You need boundless energy if you are going to make a career of campaigning.

Facts, links and trivia

Some charity organisations who use street campaigners to sign up new members offer comprehensive and professional training for its street workers. Skills in this area can be extremely useful in many other professions – being able to approach and communicate effectively with members of the public is prized in a whole host of other public facing positions. This level of training also recognises that once working full time, the majority of the campaigner's principle income will come from commission for each new member recruited. With this arrangement successful campaigners can earn around £400–£500 per week.

All the main campaign organisations have Web sites – Amnesty International can be found at www.amnesty.org, Oxfam at www.oxfam.org. For those who prefer the hands-on international approach, a particularly useful resource is www.devnetjobs.org which offers a comprehensive listing of international development jobs.

Chauffeur

If you love cars, why not drive them for a living? True, you might not get to be Nigel Mansell, but there are plenty of other ways in which to indulge your automobile fascination. People need to be driven around for many different reasons. Celebrities and VIPs are simply too important to drive themselves anywhere. You may find yourself the sole chauffeur of a particular client or working for a chauffeur company used by many different people. You could be driving them to attend important social functions or simply to the shops. Your clients may not always want to attract attention to themselves – a jobbing chauffeur is as likely to find lucrative work ferrying someone around in an unremarkable vehicle as to be forever dusting off the Bentley.

There are many occasions when general members of the public require car services. Weddings, in particular, use special chauffeur-driven vehicles – old, new and unique – to add to the important day.

You may find you need to own your own car for this job, but equally, as part of a chauffeur company, it is likely that you will share the vehicles between drivers. You will need a full, clean driving licence and special insurance to cover any accidents that may damage either the vehicle or your passengers. There are obvious financial responsibilities involved with providing your own vehicle – not simply involving purchase but upkeep as well. It will not be sufficient to make sure simply that the vehicle is roadworthy, as customers will expect a certain standard of cleanliness both inside and outside the car.

 Highs: Driving around in unusual and attractive vehicles.

 Lows: Traffic jams.

Facts, links and trivia

Browse your way through the local press and the *Yellow Pages* to suss out the local market for chauffer driven vehicles. Some companies dedicate themselves to the luxury market and may also hire out unique or performance vehicles for self-drive purposes (vehicles such as the Lamborghini Diablo are hardly going to be chauffeur driven but can command daily hire charges of around £1,000). Alternatively, companies can provide a full range of transportation – mixing the classic Rolls Royce Silver Shadow with the offering of a luxury coach to drive around parties of 30–50 people.

In New York one chauffer company has hit on a scheme that cashes in on the Americans' love of their animals. Pet Ride at www.petride.com will transport your pet any distance in comfort and safety. The company charges US $25 to drive 1–40 blocks, US $2.75 per mile outside the city and has special rates for longer distances.

Organic shopkeeper

The debate over the merit of organic, non-organic and genetically modified (GM) foods has made headlines in recent years. The rise in interest in organic and health foods is unquestionable and today the situation exists where demand for guaranteed organic produce far outstrips supply. In some cases supermarkets realising the potential of the market are exercising their buying power with organic farmers and organic produce suppliers, but there is still a place for the small, local organic shop. Indeed such enterprises, with their local focus in terms of the suppliers they use and the other businesses they support, bring far greater ecological and economical benefits to the local community and general environment than the supermarkets ever could.

Establishing a shop is, however, a mammoth task. Location is crucial to success – not simply in terms of the customers who pass through the door, but the wider neighbourhood customers who may be receptive to value added services such as door-to-door box delivery of produce. Aside from the marketing implications of this decision, you must also consider the property you are using, from the layout of the shop to the nature of the lease you are given for the property. Before you start you need to sort out how to finance the operation, who will staff the shop and so on. In general, you cannot expect a new enterprise to start paying its own way for at least three years.

Many organic produce or health food shops end up making their money on the 'pills and potions' shelf – a line of goods which includes selling vitamins, mineral supplements, herbal remedies and so on. These goods have a great mark-up price for the retailer that is often used to cover other loss making or break-even product lines. On the other hand, shops can realise profit margins through value added services such as making fresh juice and soup or running box delivery schemes.

It is a good idea to begin by working in a similar shop to see how such a store works. You will find running the shop can be a fairly mundane task – the usual requirements of stocktaking, ordering goods, receiving, pricing and selling goods is similar work to that in any shop. The difference is that organic produce is more than just another product and can be more than just a lifestyle choice. If you set up the shop carefully it will not only help to promote healthy living among its clientele, it can encourage greater environmental awareness within the locality and even help lessen the impact of 21st century living on the planet.

 Highs: Creating a business with ecological benefits.

 Lows: Setting up and running a shop is a 24-hour, 7 days a week obsession. Do not expect any other life and do not expect the business to start paying you back for at least three years.

Facts, links and trivia

The Soil Association governs organic standards and recognises organic produce. It can be contacted at Bristol House, 40–56 Victoria Street, Bristol, BS1 6BY (tel: 0117 929 0661). Its Web site www.soilassociation.org is a mine of information and includes material on manufacturing and retail. At the same time, the Farm Retail Association represents operations ranging from farm shops through to the running of box schemes. Its Web site is at www.farmshopping.com or write to The Greenhouse, PO Box 575, Southampton SO15 7ZB.

Interestingly, the government has recognised the importance of small local shops to the fabric of good neighbourhoods and society in general. Such shops provide a good community focus as well as promoting the local economy rather than simply contributing to the profits of a national or multinational operation. The Better Regulation Task Force is currently studying ways to make it easier for local shops to operate, providing the support they need and reducing the amount of bureaucracy that surrounds their operation.

Painting conservator

Removing the rigours of time from an old painting can be as much of an art as creating the painting in the first place. The most treasured masterpiece can become foul through neglect or accident – canvases may become torn and layers of dirt can build up reducing the original impact of the painting.

A painting conservator works to reverse this damage and restore the painting to something approaching its original appearance. It is both painstaking and rewarding work, requiring the conservator to apply many different treatments and techniques to the work in order to restore the painting fully. There may be many layers of varnish painted over the damage that needs to be removed. Indeed, this varnish may have to be stripped before the artwork can be retouched or more substantial damage addressed.

Painting conservation is meticulous work and requires patience and skill as well as a wealth of knowledge of the art world and restoration techniques. The bad news is that training to be a fully qualified painting conservator takes 5–10 years, a period which includes studying art, art history or natural sciences. This is followed by postgraduate training courses in which to learn specific restoration techniques as well as introducing students to the practical side of the work.

In spite of this academic requirement, it is expected that prospective conservators should also have a significant amount of practical experience on the job and such opportunities can be found through voluntary work at museums and galleries. Volunteering for this kind of work – usually as a general dogsbody, helping out a qualified conservator – can be done at any time and will give you a good idea of what the work involves before committing such a substantial amount of time to study. Fully qualified conservators may work in studios or for art institutions but it is possible to work on a freelance basis, using your own studio to carry out work on some paintings or travelling to various locations to do work on site as required.

 Highs: Being as close to a painting as the original artist.

 Lows: Scraping layers of glue off the back of a canvas with a scalpel for hours can get a bit boring.

Facts, links and trivia

The Association of British Picture Restorers (ABPR) has around 400 members (not all in Britain, however) and works to represent the industry and share best practice between restorers. Painting conservators can only get professional assessment to become a Fellow of the ABPR after seven years' experience which can include training in a studio or on a university course. The ABPR can be contacted via abprlondon@aol.com or at Station Avenue, Kew, Surrey TW9 3QA (tel: 020 8948 5644) and has a useful Web site at www.abpr.co.uk.

There is also a resource at www.conservationconsortium.com which offers conservators the chance to be included in an electronic listing/searchable address book for customers to find conservators in their geographical area. Conservators can also advise on how to preserve paintings so they will not deteriorate. While their advice includes being careful not to hang oil paintings over radiators, fireplaces or in direct sunlight, thankfully they don't actually tell you to wrap them up and put them in the loft forever.

Body piercer

Body jewellery has become extremely popular in recent years with metal and stones adorning almost every part of the human body. For some, body piercing has become an obsession – a statement about themselves or an ongoing experiment with their own bodies.

Medical groups have expressed concern about the lack of regulation in body piercing practices. While in London body-piercing studios must be registered with their local authority, practices outside the capital do not – a fairly ridiculous situation given that ear-piercing studios and tattoo parlours do need to be licensed. That said, every studio dealing in this kind of work must strictly adhere to guidelines set out in other areas of the law such as Health and Safety at Work legislation relating to sterilisation and even the use of anaesthetics as outlined in The Medicines Act dating back to 1968. Apprentices in body piercing must take full training including a reputable first aid class and a course in blood diseases. Both of these are available through organisations such as the Red Cross, the Occupational Safety Health Association or The National Safety Council.

Alongside this the piercer should spend a minimum of three months as a trainee in a piercing studio learning first hand about sterilisation, disinfection and the prevention of cross contamination. In the same way that tattooists pass on their skills to interested individuals in the next generation, qualified piercers pass their knowledge and techniques to trainees. For at least six months (depending on the number of clients dealt with by the studio) the trainee works alongside qualified staff, learning how to prepare for a piercing, using the autoclave to sterilise the piercing needles and getting the necessary consent forms signed by the client.

Training may simply be a matter of observation at first, but eventually the trainee will take on piercings, all carried out under the watchful eye of their mentor. While the technique is essentially the same for all piercings, the piercer must learn the potential dangers to the circulatory and nervous systems for each and be able to identify when a piercing is not suitable for a client.

Piercings are carried out in a sterile and safe environment, where the individual being pierced understands what is going to happen and how to look after their body jewellery after the piercing. It is extremely rare for an individual to receive training without already having access to or working for a licensed body-piercing studio. After a year or so, the trainee piercer undergoes a verbal exam covering health and safety procedures to ensure that he or she understands how to pierce safely. Having gained a certificate from the local Department of Health and Consumer Protection, the individual can pierce on his or her own.

 Highs: Giving people a very special decoration.

 Lows: Clients who pass out.

Facts, links and trivia

Body piercing is extremely vulnerable to fashion trends. While it might be all the rage to get a belly button piercing one summer, the following year it could be completely passé. Other forms of body alteration are rising in popularity among some people. Alternative dentistry involves the alteration of the teeth for cosmetic purposes. However, such radical procedures as filing, removal and the introduction of metal covering for the teeth requires initial training in conventional dentistry.

The Association of Professional Piercers started out in the United States in the late 1990s. It has a Web site at www.safepiercing.org and is the focus point for generating effective training methods to be used internationally. The European branch also has a Web site at the less succinct www.users.dircon.co.uk./~c-steel/app.html, or perhaps it's easier to write to: APP, PO Box 16044, London NW1 8ZD.

**The
Sporty
Kind**

re you good at games? Are you fit? Are you glued to the TV watching every match, race or contest you can? How about turning that passion into cash? Professional sportspeople will usually have their careers mapped out from their early–mid teenage years. They will be lined up for a life of continual training, attention to physical development, diets and discipline. This might mean you are too late to be able to battle through to the show courts of Wimbledon and you may never be picked for the national football team, but there are many other ways your passion for athletic activity can be put to good use in the workplace. You may be able to offer your talents as a coach or games official. You might find your niche in managing sports venues – anything from a sports centre to a huge stadium. You can still get a healthy kick out of your work, running around for enjoyment rather than because your boss has given you too much work to do.

Increased awareness of a healthier lifestyle has paved the way for many job opportunities in the sports sector, such as coaching, training and instructing – working out with members of the general public as well as with professional teams. There are also opportunities for those who simply cannot sit still during their working day – people with energy to burn in need of a daily challenge. So do not delay, get under starter's orders and take the plunge.

Rickshaw driver

A physical challenge with a difference – and originally a feature of oriental climes – the rickshaw is a human-powered method of transport, consisting of a cart on two wheels with two long poles that the rickshaw driver pulls. Imagine a single horse and cart, replace the horse with a human and you get the picture. Anything up to four customers can sit in the cart itself and enjoy the ride as the rickshaw driver sweats his or her way through the streets of the town in which he or she operates.

Other human-powered methods of transport are available including four-person taxi bikes enabling one cyclist to pedal passengers around town. The popularity of this and other methods of human-powered transport have increased in the UK. There is now a permanent fleet of pedal-powered taxis in London and rickshaws are also found as novelty transport during local festivals (mainly in cities that do not have extensive hills). Unsurprisingly, rickshaws tend to be more numerous during the summer months since passengers are unlikely to want to ride in quite an exposed position in winter, regardless of the feelings of the driver.

Pulling power is not the only qualification needed for this work. It is a people-oriented job which requires both charm and personality from the drivers, allowing them to shine on happily while enduring all weathers, taking orders from customers and pacifying the passing – or more likely, following – motorists. Drivers must be outgoing people since the unique selling point of the transport is its novelty value rather than its speed. Human-powered transport is always going to attract attention, so you need to be ready to exploit that attention and turn curiosity into your next fee-paying passenger.

Cycle manufacturers are continually producing new models of human-powered vehicles, many of which can be used for the transportation of packages and deliveries as well as people. Prices vary according to size and manufacturer, but you may need to shell out a few hundred pounds if you want to invest in your own set of wheels. Given this expenditure, it is worth doing a few sums to check how many miles you will have to pedal before you get your investment back. A rickshaw driver in London can charge around £40 per hour's worth of pedalling, plus tip if he or she is a particularly good driver.

Advertisements for drivers generally appear in the local press, but it is worth applying directly to any rickshaw company you come across. Obviously, you will need to have sound knowledge of the area around which you are carting people – it will be more than a little embarrassing if you have to keep asking directions from your passengers.

Highs: It's a great way to feel part of the city you are working in and to see the nightlife.

Lows: It can be dangerous negotiating traffic and high levels of pollution in built-up areas can make the work unpleasant.

Facts, links and trivia

Workbike news (www.workbike.org) is dedicated to providing news, research and resources which support the use of bicycle power in diverse working conditions. A short skip across to www.bikefix.co.uk will put you in contact with the makers of the Brox, a low-level pedal-powered vehicle that can be used on a variety of delivery jobs. This site also contains a down-loadable business plan that anyone can use as an initial outline to establish a company which uses the Brox product (www.bikefix.co.uk/i-brox_business.html).

One company currently operating in London is Bugbugs (www.bugbugs.co.uk). Its Web site not only carries personal views of the job but details training and recruitment procedures.

Cycle courier

If you get your kicks on two wheels, have the legs and stamina for biking around all day, and want to go way faster than the rickshaws, cycle couriering could be for you. Couriers can be employed as part of a complete fleet of despatch services ranging from large white vans at the top end of the scale, delivering packages across a substantial area, to motorbikes which flit through the heavily congested streets of cities, delivering smaller parcels. Each method of transport is used for its own unique qualities. The clear advantage of a cycle courier is that cyclists can go where no other vehicle can, negotiating traffic jams and taking short cuts impossible in any other method of transport. Admittedly this might not necessarily mean adhering strictly to the Highway Code at all times, but then the cycle courier is employed to get from A to B in the shortest possible time and in one piece.

The work is a great physical challenge and getting a job is usually more of a fitness test than an interview. You will need to supply your own bike and be well versed in maintaining it and ensuring it is operational at all times. Your employer will not be impressed if a delivery goes astray because you spent all day fixing a puncture. You will need to know the local streets and short cuts in detail, be prepared to continue pedalling whatever the weather and be thick-skinned when it comes to other people's appreciation of your road use. Pedestrians and motorists alike are wary of cyclists and couriers have a reputation for being particularly reckless.

Of course, if pedalling is too much like hard work, you could always be a motorbike courier. Even local pizza parlours use moped riders to get their food home-delivered while it is still hot and experience at this level would give you an idea of what it might be like when you are under greater pressure delivering important documents between businesses.

The area of home or door-to-door delivery has made a few advances recently with the introduction of dial-out services for sushi and other exotic foods. One entrepreneur took a different spin on the theme of using easy transportation to provide a mobile service to customers. If someone went out in their car and subsequently started drinking alcohol, they could phone Bikeman, a comprehensively insured and qualified driver who would come out to them on his scooter. The scooter was small enough to fit into the boot of most cars so Bikeman could then safely drive the intoxicated client back home in his or her own car.

Highs: Riding your bike and getting paid for it.

Lows: Traffic, pollution, weather, getting knocked off.

Facts, links and trivia

The city of York is thought to have the largest load-carrying fleet of cycle couriers in Europe who are reckoned to remove 150 van journeys per day from the city centre. The service may be environmentally friendly but success has only come through proving the couriers can deliver their goods faster, cheaper and more reliably than other alternatives.

While some couriers may still be taking risks as they shoot through the crowded city streets, the Department of Local Government, Transport and Regions has published 'The Courier Code', a document listing best and safe practice for couriers wherever they work and whatever they might be driving at the time. While recognising couriers tend to be self-employed and therefore must be highly skilled in order to make their living in this way, it sets out a number of ways in which cyclists can work safely, including fitting lights and a bell, and ensuring both cycle and cyclist are in a fit state to be on the road. The code is available from www.think.dtlr.gov.uk/courier. Other useful cycling-related information can be accessed via a comprehensive portal site at www.cyclist.org.uk.

Bungee jumper

One of the more bizarre leisure pursuits to emerge over the last decade has been the practice of throwing oneself from a high place when attached to something permanent only by a length of industrial strength elastic. The origins of this activity can be traced to tribesmen on the island of Vanuata in the South Pacific who started leaping off trees with vines tied to their ankles as a test of manhood. Modern Bungee jumping started at the end of the 1970s, and according to popular myth the first jump was from the Clifton Suspension Bridge in Bristol. Obviously they used elastic rather than vines.

The modern day sport retains the sense of being a rite of passage and while there have been some accidents, the majority of people who have undertaken the jump have come away feeling euphoric, even using the experience as a life-changing event, giving themselves the confidence and belief that they can do anything. It is now rare to attend a festival, fair, pop concert or similar outdoor event and not see a crane regularly lifting the next punter to a dizzying height from which to plummet.

Jumps take place all over the world, from famous bridges and impressive natural landscapes as well as from cranes. While each jump takes only seconds, the bungee jump crew are employed for days at a time to set up the equipment and supervise jumpers. It is a people-oriented activity requiring great skills in giving jumpers the reassurance they need before taking the plunge or allowing them to change their minds if they really want to.

Aside from the novelty of the act itself, however, the job can get monotonous. The Bungee Jumping company Sky High claim to be able to get in 25 jumpers per hour, and once managed to launch 220 people into the air in just one day. Like other businesses it is necessary to drum up customers, arrange venues for the activity to take place and ensure there is a constant stream of people lining up to jump. There may be special events at which bungee jumping can take place or you may find yourself catering for corporate occasions or even arranging strange requests such as couples getting married just before they jump.

 Highs: A real chance to travel, meet new people and help them jump off high platforms.

 Lows: Possibly monotonous working day – once you have seen 150 different people jumping and reacting to the jump, you've probably seen them all.

Facts, links and trivia

Any company engaging in bungee jumping activities will need insurance against accidents covering themselves for around £5 million. The British Elastic Rope Sports Association (no, really), otherwise known as BERSA (www.bersa.org), was founded to promote safety and good practice in the industry in the early 1980s. It also runs a code of safe practice drawn up in consultation with the Health and Safety Executive and an independent advisor from the Safety and Reliability Division of the UK Atomic Energy Authority. Apparently the latter organisation has knowledge and interests in high-risk entertainment activities. BERSA is based at 33A Canal Street, Oxford OX2 6BQ (tel: 01865 311179).

Paint-baller

Paint-balling consists of running around a designated area, dressed in combat gear and armed with a gun that shoots paint-balls – otherwise known as a marker. Paint-balling is usually an outdoor pursuit set in woodland or farmland sites given over to armies of paint-ballers at a particular time. In some places, there are paint-balling clubs where members dedicate some time every month to paint-balling. The sport is also popular for business and corporate entertainment, for birthdays and even for stag parties.

There are some dangers connected to the sport and customer training is always a priority before allowing contestants to set out and shoot one another. Protective clothing should be worn including special facemasks to protect the eyes from a direct hit. For some games, teams of paint-ballers will be set against each other in which case additional supervision may be required to ensure no one gets lost or hurt.

As with bungee jumping crews, day-to-day duties can seem run-of-the-mill but there is always the opportunity to create new challenges for participants and to redesign the area around which the game is played. This could mean landscaping the area or even building hideouts and shelters for players to use.

As the activity has grown in popularity, particularly in the corporate leisure market, and as regular tournaments have grown up on a national basis, the industry has witnessed a war of its own for delivering the most competitive price. Players today can expect to pay at least £20–£30 per head with a charge for extra paint-balls used of as much as 10p each. If you're going to set up your own operation you should consider the current market and assess whether your site is going to be operating in direct competition with an existing one.

Laser questing is a similar operation – the paint-ball gun is replaced with a laser gun that shoots a beam of light detected by light-sensitive receptors on each player's body. This time the game is played indoors and once again, there is the opportunity to design exciting environments around which the game can be played – playing with stage sets and atmospheric lighting, dry ice and music.

 Highs: Designing and running an exciting and physically demanding game.

Lows: You may find you play the game less as more customers take up the game.

Facts, links and trivia

Creating a new site can be costly. Not only will you need to find a suitable location, getting the right balance between interesting territory and potential death-traps – it's not a very good idea to allow a load of enthusiastic paint-ballers to run full tilt around a site with concealed ditches, for example – the equipment you buy may also be critical to popularity with your customers. A set of professional goggles can cost around £5 each with basic guns or markers starting at £100–£150. It is important, however, to get equipment which will stand up to the rigours of extended and repetitive use so markers may be more expensive.

The Web site www.paintball.co.uk provides a useful set of resource for interested paint-ballers including a search engine for sites around the UK. Meanwhile, www.paintballonline.co.uk offers online shopping for your paint-ball needs.

Diver

Professional divers work in various industries. Diving can be simply a leisure pursuit and many trainers find themselves work in holiday resorts across the world, teaching people to dive or accompanying them on trips to see the wonders of the deep. At the same time, divers are used by other seabound industries. The oil industry, for example, uses divers to carry out undersea rig inspections and maintenance work. Divers may also find work in salvage operations where goods need to be retrieved from the sea. They may even be used in an investigative capacity to discover clues as to why a vessel sank.

Learning to dive is a demanding but rewarding exercise, and can be expensive. Training courses for beginners are recognised by the Professional Association of Diving Instructors (PADI) or the British Sub-Aqua Club who can also put you in touch with your nearest diving school. The PADI Open Water course is designed for beginners, qualifying them for dives of up to 18 metres. It costs around £300 and lasts for five days. Other courses give divers qualifications in areas such as ocean diving, wreck diving and leading a dive. While you can hire equipment, if you are taking the activity seriously you will need to buy your own wet suit, air tanks and other equipment, all of which can take the cost into thousands of pounds.

Once trained, there are no easy ways to get work as a professional diver. In general, you should get in touch with some of the clients listed above and offer your services. Alternatively, the diving schools themselves may have useful employment contacts or could employ you to pass on your skills to new trainees.

The skills of divers working on industrial and commercial projects have been recognised as useful in dry land situations as well. Techniques used by offshore divers for salvage work on oil rigs or other submerged structures can be applied to situations on constructions above ground where abseiling presents the only feasible form of access. Since divers working in the industrial field will already have gained construction and maintenance skills they can easily transfer those skills to the needs of the construction industry. It is interesting to note that it only takes four days' training plus one day's independent assessment to gain the Level 1 minimum qualification for rope work, as recognised by the Industrial Rope Access Trade Association.

A **Highs:** See things other people never will.

V **Lows:** Some danger is involved with every dive.

Facts, links and trivia

A basic learn to dive course can cost around £50 per half day although this can be reduced if you join a club or learn with a group of other people. The British Sub-Aqua Club have regional centres around the UK but can be contacted at their headquarters: BSAC, Telford's Quay, South Pier Road, Ellesmere Port, Cheshire CH65 4FL (tel: 0151 3506200).

There are numerous resources and links at their Web site www.bsac.com as there are at www.ukdiving.co.uk, including a searchable database of training centres and a direct link to the Met Office's Web site for divers to check on current and future weather conditions. PADI International Ltd recognises courses around the world and is based at Unit 7, St Phillips Central, Albert Road, Bristol BS2 0XJ, www.padi.com (tel: 0117 3007234).

The Industrial Rope Access Trade Association (IRATA) can be contacted at Association House, 235 Ash Road, Aldershot, Hampshire GU12 4DD, www.irata.com (tel: 01252 336318).

Sports referee

While getting the call up to play for a major league team or as a player in an event of national and international significance may be remote, fit and talented sportspeople with a keen interest in their sport can attain a meaningful and important role in their discipline. To be successful, referees need to be as fit and as knowledgeable about their sport as every other player. Indeed, they probably need to be more knowledgeable in order to resolve disputes fairly and confidently.

Referees are usually trained by the relevant game's governing body or association. In the case of football, the Referee's Association (RA) oversees the recruitment, training and promotion of referees. The RA's initial classroom-based training course lasts for nine evenings and includes two examinations. There are local training officers contactable through each RA branch or through the local County Football Association. The tuition and examination is free but there is a small charge for registering with the County FA.

Newly qualified referees are supported through their local network and a mentoring scheme whereby a more experienced referee will coach the newcomer, identifying weaknesses and helping them develop their skills match by match. Promotion to higher league matches is achieved through a combination of assessment and the opinion of the clubs whose matches you referee. Club marks are awarded after each match and it should be noted that trying to swing the match for one club just to get extra points will not help since you will get fewer points from the other team. Promotion will only happen if you make yourself available for a large number of matches and you should always be ready to try out refereeing at a level above your own.

Of course, running round on a playing field trying to keep order over 90 minutes isn't always sweetness and light. There are bound to be occasions where you find yourself officiating in the middle of nowhere, in dreadful weather and in the shadow of hatred from one team plus their supporters because you actually awarded that entirely justified penalty which meant their opponents won – But hey! It's only a game…

 Highs: Keeping order and preserving the smooth running of increasingly important matches.

 Lows: Enduring abuse and retribution for unpopular decisions.

Facts, links and trivia

The RA has around 17,500 members in the UK and across 35 other countries. There are around 3,000 referees active at Class One level football.

You can contact the RA through its Web site at www.football-referee.org or by writing to 1 Westhill Road, Coundon, Coventry CV6 2AD, tel: 012476 601701. The British American Football Referee's Association can be reached through its Web site at www.btinternet.com/rmstangroom. The Rugby Football Union (www.rfu.org) also runs a training scheme and you can get a starter pack by phoning 0800 834551.

Those with an athletic passion should contact: UK Athletics, the sport's governing body at Athletics House, 10 Harborne Road, Edgbaston, Birmingham B15 3AA, www.ukathletics.org. Details of training and qualifications to be a judge of gymnastics can be found through the British Gymnastics Association (www.baga.co.uk) Ford Hall, Lilleshall National Sports Centre, Newport, Shropshire TF10 9MB (tel: 01952 822300).

Sports/aerobics instructor

Why not earn money while keeping fit? In today's world, more and more people are health conscious and concerned that while their lifestyle may be enjoyable it might not be too healthy. As a result, a weekly visit to the local gym provides the chance to get back in trim and to feel good before submitting to the rigours and temptations of another week.

Aerobics is only one method of keeping fit. Communal sports classes can also include kickboxing or yoga, or even focus on specific parts of the body such as the legs or abdominal muscles. If you are going to lead a class in this kind of activity you need to be extremely confident in what you are going to do, obviously super-fit – you need to talk and demonstrate at the same time – and very good with people. Very often, there will be stragglers or newcomers to the class who will need all the encouragement you can give them.

Another trend in this area is the use of the personal coach. This is someone who will work on physical activities on a one-to-one basis with clients. Clients may have a specific need or something to achieve from their exercise – building stamina or upper body strength, for example – and you will need to design a training regime tailored to those needs. Again, people skills are extremely important here, as you will need to explain how to do the exercises properly, what the exercises are designed to do and will need to offer loads of encouragement.

There are many options for entering this area of work and becoming an instructor. Many college courses cover physical education and will also give you the human biology knowledge required. At the same time, your local gym may also have some training opportunities, or even run an NVQ scheme in this area. Coaching, teaching and instructing now exists at NVQ Level 2 and is available across five disciplines: exercise to music, aqua exercise to music, step exercise to music, circuits and gymnasium.

Highs: Physical exercise produces body chemicals that make you happy!

 Lows: At first you may find yourself permanently tired out. You must also be aware that instructors are as susceptible to injury as other professional sportspeople. Without proper insurance against this, you could have a mishap which ends your lucrative career.

Facts, links and trivia

Sports Aerobics was officially recognised by the Federation International de Gymnastics Congress in Atlanta in 1995 and Great Britain won the Bronze Medal for Mixed Pairs at the World Games in Finland 1997. A booklet detailing the sport and competition is available from the British Gymnastics Association (www.baga.co.uk) or Ford Hall, Lilleshall National Sports Centre, Newport, Shropshire TF10 9MB (tel: 01952 822300).

Single personal sessions can last from 45 minutes upwards (depending on the needs of the clients) and can net wages of at least £30. Qualified instructors should be officially registered with the Fitness Industry Association (www.fia.org.uk) 115 Eastbourne Mews, Paddington, London W2 6LQ (tel: 020 7298 6730). Further support and recognition can be gained from other industry organisations including the Association of Personal Trainers, Suite 2, 8 Bedford Court, London WC2E 9OU (tel: 020 7836 1102) the Aerobics and Fitness Organisation of Great Britain (AFOGB) Unit 9, Station Road Business Park, Station Road, Barrack, Stamford, Lincolnshire PE9 3DW (tel: 01780 749009), while recognised training courses in movement and dance are also run by Keep Fit Association, Francis House, Francis Street, London SW1P 1DE (tel: 020 7233 8898) www.keepfit.org.uk.

Stadium groundsperson

There is more to looking after a sports pitch than watering and cutting the grass every so often. Growing grass for sports purposes has become an exact science. The truly proficient groundsperson needs to understand the effects of rainfall, of sunshine and of atmospheric conditions on the turf. This has become all the more important as venues have increased the number of fixtures they have each season. Fresh demands are also made of the pitch's turf as sports arenas play host to non-sporting events such as rock concerts and rallies.

Some venues now use movable turf in order to enable other events to take place without damaging the pitch. Synthetic grass is not popular among footballers, so the current trend is to create a 'live' pitch on a series of pallets that can then be moved when the occasion demands. These pallets present their own problems in terms of ensuring sufficient drainage to produce healthy turf. Even building technology has created new challenges for turf specialists with removable roofs offering the choice of protecting the pitch from the elements.

While this change in the management of pitches has led to the introduction of some very specialist courses in turf technology, the simplest way into grounds work is through voluntary work. You may not be paid and the work could be extremely mundane for a while, but by being there, you will learn how to look after the turf all year round. In addition, some colleges will only accept students who have a proven interest in this area and already have practical experience of looking after a pitch.

Groundspeople are used worldwide. In the United States there are even agencies dedicated to assigning highly experienced staff to well-known venues across the country – golf courses and luxury hotel grounds – as well as football and baseball pitches. The work itself is more painstaking than demanding. There may be some heavy manual work to be done but it is more about knowing how to treat a pitch or field. Ground staff must know when to tend the turf and how to repair damage inflicted during use. This can be quite a high pressure job in some cases since events such as Wimbledon or major football matches will be televised and have national and international significance. Any suggestions that the ground is not in tip-top condition will not only look bad for the venue but could cause problems for the image of the game across the world.

 Highs: Achieving a perfect playing surface for an important event.

 Lows: Irregular hours.

Facts, links and trivia

The Web site www.sprito-els.org.uk provides an excellent portal into employment, learning and skills required throughout the sports industry. SPRITO is the industry body created by employers and industry bodies to develop vocational qualifications and standards across the industry. Its head office is at 24–32 Stephenson Way, London NW1 2HD (tel: 020 7388 7755).

While Wembley Stadium is being redeveloped, the closest you're likely to get to the hallowed turf is at www.wembleynationalstadium.co.uk or alternatively you can find out about the diverse music and sports fixtures appearing at the Millennium Stadium in Wales at www.cardiff-stadium.co.uk.

Demolition person

It may seem to be a little backwards but in order to be a decon-struction expert one must first gain qualifications with the Construction Industry Training Board. On the other hand, this makes perfect sense: taking down a building safely can only be done with an understanding of how construction works – how buildings fit together. Attacking a wall randomly in a block of flats with a sledgehammer is unlikely to have the desired effect.

Demolition operatives start their careers with a demolition company and undergo training on the job. This training covers safety on site, accident prevention and personal safety, the control of asbestos and lead and even the control of noise pollution. The trainee will also learn how to prevent fires occurring and how to react if they do. At this stage, the trainee will have nothing to do with any machinery and will certainly not be given a load of explosives to set and detonate. These are specialist areas that require a good deal of on-site experience and additional training.

Before demolition takes place, the workers need to assess the materials which will be produced by the deconstruction and decide how these materials will be handled. Measures are taken to control the dust created during the demolition process and hazardous materials require special packing. Demolition workers could find themselves dealing with relatively low level hazards in areas such as urban renewal, but other contracts might involve cleaning up chemicals and dealing with other environmentally unfriendly waste products.

Plant machinery such as specially equipped JCBs and diggers are often used to cut through reinforced concrete or iron supports and operating this kind of equipment requires a good deal of training. Blowing up a building is a strategic job. Explosive experts must set the right charges at the right loca-tions in a building; perhaps removing supporting walls to ensure the building comes down first time. The explosion must be planned carefully so that the building comes down in the right area – there could be other buildings nearby which it would be a good idea to leave standing at the end of the day. There may also be electricity power lines or sewers underneath the building that must not be damaged by the blast.

However the building is brought down, safety is always the prime consideration for both the individuals working on site and for the general public. The demolition operative must therefore be able to work responsibly within a team and be able to take the initiative in order to reduce hazards as the demolition progresses.

 Highs: Regenerating land for reuse.

 Lows: Hard manual labour in order to gain responsibilities.

Facts, links and trivia

You can view some intriguing guidelines on the Web site from the Health and Safety Executive titled: 'Establishing Exclusion Zones when using Explosives in Demolition' held at www.hse.gov.uk/pubns/cis45.htm.

Controlled Demolition Group Ltd is a UK company with an international range of clients and a great site that covers their work and the industry at www.controlled-demolition.co.uk. Make sure you play the entertaining introduction page! This site also has links to the half dozen industry bodies that represent demolition workers in the UK and Europe. The Construction Industry Training Board's Web site is at www.citb.org.uk or you can write to them at Bircham Newton, King's Lynn, Norfolk PE31 6RH (tel: 01485 577577).